Testimonials

Amy pushes traditional leadership thinking in a digital and global age, where quality conversations and communication is the single biggest challenge faced by leaders. No matter where you are - or think you are - on your leadership journey, Amy will give you the required empathy bump to help you continually evolve and have constant and authentic 'clicking' conversations.

Marnie Shervey, Executive Product Manager, IRESS

Amy's insights into the positive impact that people managers and leaders can, and do, have are powerful. Too often, leaders take on the role of commander as opposed to servant. People leaders that understand and embrace opportunities to be of service to their teams are the ones that often see greater levels of curiosity and accountability, and benefit from greater engagement as a result. Amy's exploration is a must read for people leaders highlighting the role we play is both a privilege and responsibility to create an environment that inspires growth.

Elizabeth Bardwell, Head of Communications, Australia and Digital Banking, ANZ

When I read a book I look for three things: 1) easy and enjoyable to read, 2) stretches my thinking (and makes me a little uncomfortable!), and 3) provides practical advice I can implement. Dr Amy Silver's new book 'Conversations Create Growth' does all three - and more! As leaders, we spend so much of our day taking, but how many of those conversations really make a difference? For smart people who want to influence others to give their best, here's the map with 3 insider secrets from psychology to help people grow just by talking!

Corrinne Armour, Leadership Speaker, Trainer, Coach

In this new world of communication by digital means, "Conversations Create Growth" reintroduces us to the important element of conversations, and how they can shape the dynamic of our teams, and leave an indelible message for your people. By delving into key issues on a personal basis, albeit challenging and confronting at times, the book provides valuable lessons in developing connection for the benefit of both the individual and the organisation. I encourage all managers who wish to practice exceptional leadership qualities to inspire others, develop advocates for the business and drive tangible outcomes, to refer to Dr Silver's new book, and apply the practical examples of maximising team performance.

Martin Goodrich, Partner, Crowe Horwath & Centric Wealth

Brilliantly written and guaranteed to get the attention of anyone who is serious about leadership and self-improvement. This book has you captured in the moment whilst simultaneously reflecting on every important conversation you've had and asking what could you have said differently, and what could the outcome have been. It teaches you the importance of your words and has some essential learnings for all people leaders.

Darren Banfield, Executive Director, Lawson Delaney

There is no manual for each individual with whom we work or lead. The most complex, most critical role we have as a leader is to navigate our way through daily conversations and engagements on the hope that we are enabling them. We so often can be constrained by corporate processes and rules that often inhibit real conversations. With this book Amy maps out for you how to build your capability to inspire and guide to help your team grow, which of course means changing the behaviours of oneself. This is the guide book for leaders seeking growth and human connection through better conversations.

Deanna Lomas, Chief Supply Chain Officer, Super Retail Group

conversations
create growth

conversations
create growth

how to propel the performance of those
you manage, EVERY time you meet

dr. amy silver

© Dr. Amy Silver 2017

First published in 2017 by Baker Street Press | Melbourne

ISBN 978-0-9943214-7-3

This book uses case studies to enforce the meaning
behind its relevant chapters. Names have been omitted
or changed to protect individual privacy.

Every effort has been made to trace (and seek permission for use
of) the original source of material used within this book. Where
the attempt has been unsuccessful, the publisher would be pleased
to hear from the author/publisher to rectify any omission.

National Library of Australia Cataloguing-in-Publication entry
Creator: Dr. Silver, Amy, author.
Title: Conversations create growth: how to propel the performance
of those you manage, every time you meet
/ written by Dr. Amy Silver; Edited by Joanna Yardley.
ISBN: 9780994321473 (paperback)
Notes: Includes bibliographical references.
Subjects: Personnel management.
Communication in personnel management.
Management.
Leadership.
Interpersonal relations.
Other Creators/Contributors:
Yardley, Joanna, editor.

Contents

Preface

Conversations are our tool for growth

My role as a clinical psychologist, in the National Health Service in the UK, was to have conversations that created growth. People would arrive at my office after being referred by a medical professional. These patients suffered from a range of conditions including depression, personality disorders, anxiety or intolerable feelings of anger or shame. They would present with behaviours that were not helpful to either themselves or their loved ones. These behaviours included drinking, avoidance of people or places or activities, self-harm, difficulties with maintaining healthy weights, perfectionism, over-criticalness, overwhelming frustration, obsessive compulsive behaviours, health anxieties and other self-sabotaging or aggressive behaviours. I worked with people who suffered for long periods and/or in a very acute way. My purpose was to help them engage with life in a more helpful way, and drive their quality of life higher. Mostly, I had very little influence over the reality of what had brought the patient to their current place. I had one hour a week; that's one, one-hour conversation; a total of 16 hours, the maximum the NHS would cover in my clinic. People arrived holding very rigid beliefs about the world, themselves and others. The challenge was to have conversations that could lead to changing their unhelpful behaviours. Most of the time, thankfully, we saw significant life changes—conversations create growth.

Of course, although we had only 16 hours of conversations, there were 2,688 hours in total (if we assume we were in a relationship for the full 16 weeks). Our conversations were a pause in their week, an opportunity to reflect and reset, to practice and prepare, and to increase awareness and activation. That is the power of a conversation. The patients had to put in the work; they were the ones doing the hard work to change; they were the ones taking the risks and dealing with failures; they were the ones who were tenacious, brave and resourceful. I took pleasure in their achievements, and I was privileged to witness their growth. I knew their histories, their pain, the rigidity of their thinking and the entrenched behavioural habits that existed before we met. I knew the hard work of showing up to those conversations, the hard work of completing the reflections and 'homework' we had constructed, the books they had read at my request, the diaries they had completed, the personal histories they had written, the risks they had taken and the vulnerability they owned. I knew how they had continued the conversations we had into activation, into conversations with other people in their lives, into new habits and into behavioural experiments.

Through our conversations, their tasks and their goals were built, and they started to bravely experiment. Conversations were our way to assess and adjust our actions, either within our experiments or in our relationship. Just like the way we measure the slope of our shelves with a spirit level, we measure the balance of our relationships with conversations. Without knowing how balanced things are, without adjusting accordingly, things start to fall off the shelf. Ineffective conversations will reduce our capability to influence each other.

When I moved into the corporate world, the behaviours I witnessed were different. My role, however, was the same. I would help people grow, and stretch who they were so they could be more engaged with and more proud of what they did. The focus was to close the gap between their potential and their performance.

Many people use conversations effectively to create wonderful opportunities for growth for their colleagues. But I still see too many unhelpful, sometimes damaging conversations, and an even larger number of absent conversations, which have dramatic and long-term implications for a person's capacity to grow, either in engagement or performance. Conversations between people at work, even between leaders, are often unengaging, misleading or just plain missing the point. The decades of hierarchy in institutions has taken effect and left us with politics, bias, inauthenticity and fear. We have, to some extent, become reliant more on process and less on human communication.

The quantity of quality conversations predicts our sustainable growth. Conversations are our tool to assess and adjust our relationships, our engagement, and our performance. Not only do relationships and conversations determine growth around an individual's behaviour and satisfaction, but they absolutely and fundamentally determine business growth and tangible returns.

This book is an exploration of how we activate growth, how we help someone grow just by talking to them, and how can you serve others so you create growth in every conversation you have.

Acknowledgements

Not all conversations are equal. I will be forever grateful for the conversations I have had with Austin Sellyn, my children, Kirstin Eccles, Professor Adrian Wells, Professor Chris Main, my parents and sister, Corrinne Armour, Jane Anderson, Peter Cook and Matt Church. Thank you.

I am grateful to those people who have come to me with a goal of growth; thank you for trusting me enough to be part of it—it is a privilege I cherish.

Introduction

I strongly believe we should push ourselves to constantly grow; to see what we can achieve; to establish that of which we are truly capable. I feel this as a core value, something I believe I have a responsibility to do, to push myself to see what is possible to achieve with my brain and body. Sometimes I do this endurance-wise, for example, 'I wonder if I could run 15 km', and sometimes I do it mentally 'I wonder if I could focus on task X exclusively for 30 minutes'. I also set challenges, 'I want to be able to hold a room of 5000 people for a 45-minute talk', or 'I want to start working with a client in X industry', or 'I want to let go of day- to-day management of X'. These are all examples of targets that require me to grow in order to complete them. I need to be able to change my default, change my habits.

The problem with humans is that we are creatures of habit; we don't like change. We don't like shifting our patterns of behaviour or our patterns of thinking. Our fear of failure and our fear of rejection keep us rigid, even when fluidity is more sensible. Our lives often become limited by habit and expectation. When you spend a lot of time doing the same thing, or with a fixed group of people, your expectations of yourself and others' expectations of you become fixed; they keep you trapped.

When we visit other cities or countries, or even when we change jobs or relationships, we have the opportunity to surround ourselves with new people and places that enable us to have a fluidity to our behaviours and thoughts. For example, if I lived in a city foreign to me for a period of six months, I'd have the opportunity to change. I would be in charge of my choices and behaviour because I would not be running it through the filter of my existing circumstances with my existing relationships. This *fluidity of self* has always interested me, the capacity that we have to be able to change not only what we do, but how we think and ultimately who we choose to be. Assuming we only have one life, the idea that we become more rigid rather than continue to grow, seems so strange to me.

Some of the patients I worked with when I was a clinical psychologist, particularly those who were adapting to loss or trauma, had no choice but to learn to live with their new histories or circumstances. For example, I worked with people who had experienced spinal trauma leading to paralysis, or people who had bodies that had been drastically changed in other ways: burns, scarring or loss of body parts. I worked with people who had been in accidents or abusive situations, wars and horrible acts of aggression. All these patients had to deal with changes to their levels of functioning, and changes in their self-expectations and the expectations of others. Their lives were changed forever.

Our task was to help people adapt to their new physical or behavioural presentations, to grow through their, most often, unchosen circumstance. It is thankfully unimaginable to most people what might happen for individuals, post-trauma. The implications of the changes that people experienced were far reaching. People were affected in terms of their occupations and financial circumstances, family relationships, future relationships, sense of vulnerability and their feelings about rights and justice. The lives of many were changed forever, and my role was to help them develop their strength, quality of life, wellbeing, and their sense of identity and worth.

Not for one moment would I suggest that experiencing change in this way is at all welcomed. However, as an observer and clinician, I am astounded at the capabilities of our brains. The people I worked with were indeed able to grow around their circumstances and define their new selves. They were able to shift and adapt rigid beliefs and behaviours. They were able to sidestep their expectations of self, and the expectations that others had of them. They found new ways to be. I love that expression about being like a tea bag, *we don't know how strong we are till we are put in hot water*. These people were a constant reminder to me of the strength of humanity, and our capability to flex and grow, and I feel so very privileged to have witnessed this for hundreds of people.

In 2000, the UK's Channel 4 aired a series called *Faking It*. The show took an individual with a particular behavioural style and trained them in a skill with which they had no previous experience. The skill would be a total antithesis of the behavioural style they routinely adopted. For example, they taught a very upper-class man to be a street graffiti artist; an IT programmer (web surfer) to be a wave surfer, having never stood on a board; and a burger van owner to be a chef of a Michelin Star restaurant. Over a period of six weeks, the subject was mentored on everything they needed in order to present to a panel of judges and attempt to 'fake it'. The panel was asked to spot the fake from a group of three, which included two experienced and skilled performers in that field.

As an example, in one episode a punk-rock musician, Chris Sweeney, was taught to be a classical orchestra conductor. The episode started with a description of Chris's current behavioural presentation—in this case, a young man who, in every way, held a stereotypical image of a punk musician. Chris was leather-clad with a bright pink mohican, had a very thick regional accent and was portrayed as a disaffected youth. He was introduced to a professor from Imperial Music College, London. Again, this man had the behavioural style that goes with everything you would expect from a professor, including a very strong upper-class accent, wearing a shirt and tie at home, corduroy trousers, the lot—totally opposite to Chris. The professor tutored Chris for six weeks on the art and science of classical music, and the skill of conducting. During those six weeks, Chris lived with the professor and his family. At the end of the program, Chris was to conduct on one song with a full-sized orchestra in front of a full audience at a state concert auditorium. The pair's task was to enable Chris to fake it as a professional conductor to the panel of judges and the audience.

The transformation was enormous. Chris learnt incredible technical skills. However, it was the emotional and cognitive struggles that he experienced in adapting to his new environment that were so transformative—life-changing, in fact. The impact of living with a family along with their belief and commitment in him had a huge impact on his journey to change. Chris experienced frustration with his own learning, and his ability to change and adapt, and continually had to combat his desire to give in, give up and walk away. During the six weeks he started to replay his previous attempts to better himself and grow, and the many ways in which he had been undermined or failed. The result of this very difficult six-week experiment was a shift in his values, his desires, and his goals, as he experienced the options of different ways to live, different music to listen to and the different relationships he might be able to have.

When he finally stood in front of the concert orchestra to perform, he looked the part with a new 'conventional' haircut and black-tie suit. To the untrained ear, and most of the audience, he appeared skilled and knowledgeable.

Although Chris made one small, undeniable error, which the judges used to determine he was the fake, he received the largest applause from the audience that night. Chris's transformation was captivating to watch, and beautifully demonstrated the fluidity we all have.

The Channel 4 series, which had 48 episodes, took many people from different walks of life and showed them how to stretch themselves into new ways of being. The task of 'faking it' with the judges was for the TV program, and of course it was edited to create drama. But despite all that, for me, it was an utter joy to watch people go through a supportive experiment, being changed forever in a way they just hadn't thought possible. How amazing are humans!

I was glued to the series, and it had a profound impact on me. I think it was part of the inspiration that led me to become addicted to discovering what was possible when we challenge ourselves on our expectations and goals. In 2003, I left my job at Oxford University to go to drama school. During my time there, I did things I never imagined I would do; my body moved in ways it hadn't since I was a child (pretending to be a giraffe for a whole term does that to you); I developed a faith in my ability to experiment, play, and pretend—it was an incredible experience. I met a group of people with whom I fell in love; they were full of incredible intellect, creativity and courage, tenacity and dedication. A whole world of opportunity opened up to me as I began to shed some of the restrictions I had placed on myself throughout my life.

Acting also introduced me to corporate training, which is where my third career started, and where we will begin. Since 2004, I have been involved in helping people grow at work. I have worked with people, teams and businesses who strive for growth and are eager to use the lessons that I learnt in psychology and performance. My clients stretch into previously elusive behaviours, and by having 'under the surface' conversations that trigger activation, they achieve exponential growth.

I have been helping people play a bigger game, helping people surpass their expectations of self, for a very long time. Malcolm Gladwell (2008), in his book *Outliers,* discusses the importance of giving 10,000 hours to the deliberate practice of a skill if you wish to be a master. My 10,000 hours (plus a whole heap more!) is in having *conversations that create growth*.

ONE

Why should we focus on people growth?

Growth in the context of the corporate space has two meanings. First, it covers growth of *the business,* that is, revenue, profit, customers serviced, customer satisfaction, ROI etc. Second, it covers the growth of *the people in* the business, their ability, capability, wellbeing and sense of community. This growth will enable higher performance, with greater satisfaction and passion. To me, the two are different sides of the same coin. When you lead, your role is to enable your direct reports to grow in terms of their contribution to the growth of the business, and in terms of their personal growth.

So, what do we care about in terms of growth of people at work? Zenger and Folkman (2017) highlighted seven behaviours that most managers are looking for in those who perform well. You may use this list as a guide to the areas in which you want your colleagues to grow, if you are looking for a starting point:

1. *Delivering results* – the ability to provide good quality work and achieve goals on schedule.

2. *Being a trusted collaborator* – the ability to be great communicators, capable of creating trusting relationships and co-operating in groups delivering trustworthy decisions.

3. *Having strong technical/professional expertise* – the ability to keep growing technical/professional expertise to enable the organisation to excel.

4. *Translating vision and strategy into meaningful goals* – the ability to see their individual role as part of the company strategy and how to contribute to its success.

5. *Marketing your work well* – the ability to influence through 'selling' your worth.

6. *Speed* – the ability to understand information, make decisions and influence quickly.

7. *The ability to inspire and motivate others.*

You may of course want to add your own to the list. For example, I worked with a director who added 'personal satisfaction' as a growth area for his colleagues. Another added 'self-belief' as a growth area for her direct report. Growth doesn't always have to be progress in producing more, it can sometimes be progress in doing less. Many people I have worked with benefit from growth in mindfulness or self-care, creating thinking time or developing acceptance. In fact, some of the best managers I know have holistic wellbeing as a key focus for their colleagues.

You may also prefer not to drive it in any of these predetermined areas until you have discovered it together through conversation—you might have picked up already that would be my recommendation, and this book will show you how to do that.

Whose responsibility is growth?

Of course self-direction, and to some extent time and experience, will provide growth for individuals. We expect that people will be focused on their own growth, that they will strive for betterment of themselves, their lives, their work and their colleagues. This is true in many cases and at many times. Self-desire will undoubtedly make growth happen.

However, how much more could someone grow with the right opportunities? As a people manager, you are one of the tools that a person has to enable their growth. You are certainly not everything, and we know how important leadership, culture, resources, projects, and even luck are in contributing to their growth. The question that I want to encourage you to hold in your mind is how much of your direct reports' growth can *you* contribute to? Wouldn't it be great if you could maximise what you can contribute to? How much more fun is it to feel we are influencing and enabling others to be their best?

I hope it is clear to you by now that I believe if you are a people manager, maximising growth is your role. And so, growth conversations should be a large part of what you do. It requires a mindset of service, a mindset that sees the people manager as serving our direct reports by creating opportunities for growth. If you are reading this book, it is likely that I am preaching to the converted. Harvey S Firestone (Molinaro, 2016) famously said, 'The growth and development of people is the highest calling of leadership'.

We must take every opportunity to help our direct reports grow. It requires ongoing commitment, and of course we have times when we wane in our leadership, or when we work with certain people our drive to contribute to growth wanes. We will need to pull ourselves back to our responsibility if we are to drive better actions. Taking responsibility, as a contributing people manager, and having great growth conversations will mean you don't only create growth for others, but you create growth for yourself. People want to be inspired, they want to understand how to grow and what it is that stops them. They want support with their efforts. Their success is your success, not only in performance indicators but in terms of having a human influence to better the quality of lives. Contributing to growth is the rewarding part of leadership.

Are you willing and able (all the time)?

Your capability to contribute to the growth of another person, and through them, and to the growth of the business, depends on whether you are willing and able.

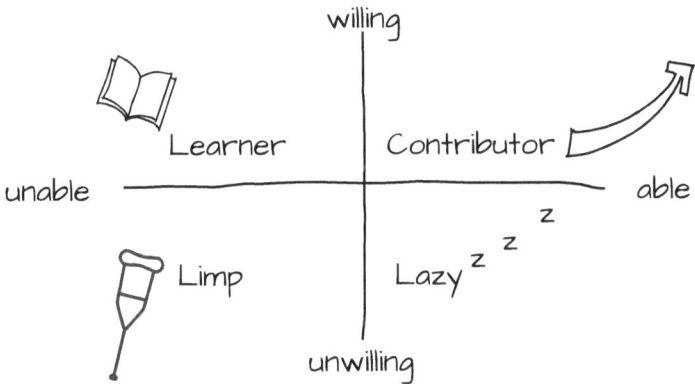

Figure 1: States of people management

The contributor state

When in this state, a people manager is both willing and able to help others grow, and therefore is a powerful contributor to that growth. I often ask people in training programs to think of someone who has contributed to their own growth. The smiles that appear show the impact those managers have had, even if the relationship was decades ago. They represent the true leader, not the hierarchical leader. Others want to follow these leaders. We follow people like this because they inspire and challenge us to grow and to give our best. They show us why and how to improve and they support us in getting there. In this state, the manager is curious, open and able to have challenging conversations with the ultimate aim of growth. They stay fresh with knowledge, ideas and practice.

Which managers have been contributors to your growth, and why?

The learner state

Sometimes we want to contribute to our direct reports' growth but for various reasons we might not have growth as an immediate focus. People managers must have the ability to change poor behaviours and foster good ones. But in certain circumstances they may lack experience, knowledge or a belief in their ability or 'place' to intervene. Perhaps they are focused on competing work metrics, distracted by work pressures or are not feeling supported or inspired themselves, and this impacts on their ability to focus on others. When in this state, the manager is likely to be less engaged themselves, perhaps experiencing distress or stress.

Often, in this state, the manager is driven to fix problems themselves and may, therefore, take on too much and focus less on building others' capability, and more on task management. Perhaps they are driven to being liked, and this can lead them to protect people from challenges that would serve them better in the longer term. In this state, the people manager is underused as a growth agent. We can easily harness the willingness that this manager has to enable growth by improving their capability in having conversations that create growth. If we show them how to challenge and trigger activation in others, they can quickly move to the contributor quadrant.

What is it like to be managed by someone caught in the Learner state?

The lazy state

Unwilling but able people managers have checked out. They would be able to help develop their team but they won't prioritise it. There is inattention to their direct reports' growth, and those in their team are viewed as widgets rather than humans. Understandably, this is incredibly disengaging for the direct reports. From my experience, this not only impacts the direct report but many people around them—sometimes, whole cultures.

It is not uncommon to find people managers caught in this lazy state. Either they are too prioritised on their individual technical skills, or perhaps are not paying attention to the future as it doesn't involve them. There is an old Greek proverb: 'A society grows great when old men plant trees whose shade they know they shall never sit in'. This lazy state is where the manager has pulled focus inwards and stopped planting trees. I often work with HR colleagues who are challenged by the desire to encourage strong leadership cultures, but a few of the executive leadership team don't actually care about the growth of people in their team. How frustrating to know that these leaders could be considerable creators of growth.

Have you ever experienced or seen a people manager who has tuned out of taking responsibility for their direct reports?

The limp state

Sometimes managers are unwilling and unable to action growth in their direct reports. These managers perhaps have found themselves in roles in which they are not interested, or with people they don't care about. Sometimes this is poor recruitment, or perhaps it is related to a promotion on technical strength without demonstrated capability of leadership. This state of people management is exhibited when the personal gain has not been understood, or the gains are not deemed relevant. They are unfocused on the growth of their direct reports, and their energy saps those who they are supposed to be leading. Their damage is widespread and can leak out to customers, clients, suppliers, and the brand. Like a limp biscuit dunked for too long, it ruins a good cup of tea!

Have you ever witnessed a people manager in this limp state?

I have mapped out these over-simplified states of people management as a reminder to you to choose where you want to sit. I have labelled them as state (rather than trait) as a reminder to you that you can get drawn into any of these quadrants at any time. If I asked you which you were, you would undoubtedly put yourself in the top half, but there will be times when you are drawn down or away from the contributing state. Different times, different people, different tasks, different leadership, different life circumstances, different periods of your life, will all have the potential to pull you away from that top right quadrant. What variables encourage you to move one way or the other? It is interesting to start thinking about what makes you shift in your willing and able variants. Can you use that clarification to help you become a better leader? What do you need to do to make sure that in every conversation you are in the top right quadrant, a contributor to growth?

As Vince Molinaro (2016) says 'Leadership is a decision, and you have to deliberately make it'. Once aware of these quadrants, my advice would be to spot yourself, increase your meta-awareness of where you are at any given conversation, and see what you can build on to push yourself up and to the right.

Retention and engagement

Why do people change jobs? In a recent survey released by Hays (2017), 61% of respondents said the number one reason people look for another job is for more challenging or exciting work. Some 60% cited a lack of career development as a main reason for them leaving, 58% cited the opportunity to improve salary, and 54% attributed it to work/life balance. This points to some of the goals that we should be working on with our own direct reports if we want to contribute to their growth, and if we want to retain them.

We don't want retention at the expense of engagement either. Gallup's January 2017 report found that engagement continues to be a major problem for most companies, with 67.5% of employees being disengaged at work. Poor drive and hampered efficiency cannibalises business growth. Compared with disengaged teams, engaged teams show 24-59% less turnover, 10% higher customer ratings, 21% greater profitability, 17% higher productivity, 28% less shrinkage, 70% fewer safety incidents and 41% less absenteeism (Gallup, 2017)

The loss of focus and commitment caused by disengagement is clear, and it spreads like a virus. Of course, there is the additional weighty cost of sick leave and performance management, the cost of re-hires and bringing a new person up to speed, and the inevitable knock-on effect to the clients and their service.

We must be able to engage a workforce and keep efficiencies high. Organisations and leaders who do not focus on growing their direct reports' performance and engagement will be inefficient. At worst, businesses that do not know how to communicate effectively in the area of growth will become irrelevant, as employees use their feet to vote away from antiquated corporates and into other opportunities.

How engaged will your colleagues be in the future?

A recent paper by Deloitte states that people entering the workforce now '...won't want to work at a place that is not cutting edge or doesn't give them the chance to learn, grow and innovate' (Deloitte, 2016). The McCann Worldgroup surveyed 7000 individuals aged between 16 and 30, and found that more than 90% of those surveyed rated 'connection and community' as their greatest need (McCann Worldgroup, n.d.). The younger generations demand growth and engagement.

Not only do we need to think about how to grow younger generations, we must also find ways to capitalise on their knowledge and expertise, on their thinking and 'culture'. They are, of course, digital 'natives' and will think in a way that *is* the future. Digital natives will behave differently in business; if current leaders don't tap into this quickly, they will be left behind.

There are already powerful digital tools that increase the power of people much lower down the business hierarchy in a way previously unseen. I recently gave a talk called *Trust* to an audience working in professional services. I mentioned *Glassdoor*, an app where employees rate their employer/organisation anonymously—like TripAdvisor for employers. I noticed from the stage, a group of young professionals who started to whisper and giggle. I asked them whether this was a sign of recognition and they said their firm had just discovered their company's unfavourable profile on the app. Leaders had previously been unaware of how much damage it was doing to their brand. Of course, the younger employees of the business had been fully aware for some time. Interestingly, the audience that day was made up of mostly older and senior employees of professional services firms. The majority of them had not heard of Glassdoor, even though most of their organisations would have a profile and ratings. This app will become more noticeable over time, and other apps will continue to emerge. How will you, as a senior leader, stay in touch with what is mainstream for the younger population? Conversations!

Several years ago, I had a future-focused client who wanted to run a series of workshops that would enable all staff to converse with a focus on technology innovation. The executive team felt so out of touch with the digital culture, and understood the valuable resource they had within their own workforce and the insights that the younger people had into technology platforms. Through facilitated conversations, we created opportunities for innovation, shared goals, cultural 'buzz', and of course, a whole heap of engagement and activated projects. Conversations created opportunities for growth of business, performance, and engagement. Organisations that underestimate the importance of increasing the conversations between generations are not only missing opportunities for growth, but relevance in the future.

As organisations become flatter, global, capitalise on outsourcing, or move to matrix systems, our ability to communicate effectively becomes even more important. Ineffective conversations, or worse, the absence of conversations, waste time and energy, and lead to ineffective and inauthentic cultures. Is it any surprise that we disengage in these cultures? That our performance stagnates? We need to improve our growth conversations so we can help bring out the best in each other, get more done quickly and with more pleasure.

Assessing professional growth

How we effectively assess our colleagues' professional growth has been a struggle for the workplace.

Having yearly performance reviews is a common way for work cultures to assess and plan for professional growth, even though there is no evidence that they help. In performance reviews, we often have a setup which encourages fear and disappointment, wrapped up in a stiff process driven by secret offline conversations with unclear content. They have the capacity to disengage not only the receiver, but the 'doer' too. I was listening to a partner who was lamenting at having to remind his direct reports of their goals. I pointed out to him that rather than this being a reflection of low motivation on his direct reports' side, it may be a reflection of the effectiveness of the conversations that he had been having across the year. How many quality conversations around growth had he had?

High-tech, low-touch solutions that enable tracking of performance are starting to appear routinely in companies. They provide the collection of data easily, and potentially enable change through high frequency prompts. These data points should mean we have more opportunity to track change, but it also has the unintentional side effect of reducing the need to converse.

In some ways it may increase the likelihood of drawing managers into a lazy state. The manager can become passive in their own measurement of the growth and their role in changing it, deferring responsibility of tracking outcome to the platform. Although there is more 'data', we bring in another layer of communication, potentially blocking growth. Unless managers understand how to have effective conversations, conversations are reduced to the outputs of the platform. This will create distance between the manager and their direct report; thereby, disabling growth.

There are many ways to track change, and whichever is used will be dependent on many cultural decisions. However, the key to this is that the process chosen must not become more important than the conversation. In fact, I am often brought into a company after they install such a system, at great cost, exactly because the success of the implementation relies on the ability of the colleagues to have conversations of growth. The platform should merely be a tool to aid conversations of growth, and yet organisations invest in them as if it were the whole solution.

Rather than the performance review being used as a six-monthly or yearly space to determine growth areas or to give feedback, they could work as a review of the effectiveness of the conversations between the manager and the direct report over that period. How effectively has the manager contributed to growth?

This reminds us all year that ongoing growth conversations are key to the development of people (performance and engagement) and business.

TWO

Growth conversations

A growth conversation is any conversation that enables your direct report to grow, either in terms of their performance or their engagement. We often assume that because we are talking, we are having conversations. But not all conversations have equal impact. Every conversation we have gets us closer or further away from our goals, and is therefore, a key driver in creating (or detracting from) high performance and engagement.

Conversation type

Remember Newton's cradle, the office toy with swinging pendulum spheres? Can you hear that satisfying and regular click, click, click? When they fall out of sync, momentum and energy are lost and the swinging starts to diminish. When they clash and tangle, the result is a mess. Conversations follow the same pattern, they can be satisfying and regular—click, click, click—or tangle into clunk, clash, cut!

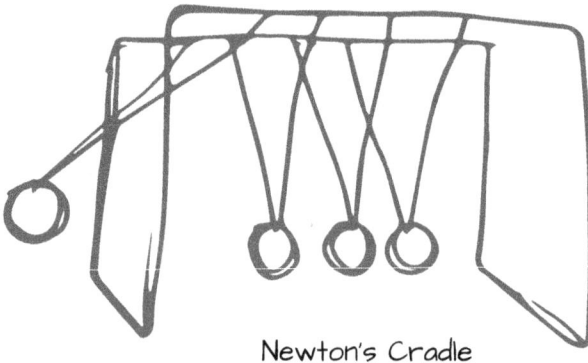

Newton's Cradle

Figure 2: Good conversations are satisfying and regular like a pendulum swing

Click

Conversations that click are welcomed, satisfying and seen as an opportunity to check in with each other about wants and desires, and what is needed to progress. There is a level of authentic communication that builds trust, creates real tracking of performance, and provides mentoring around strategies to reach goals. There is a regularity that enables a rhythm to this conversation, and both parties are safe and clear about the progress even when the content is challenging. Sound nice?

Clunk

This is how I describe conversations between a manager and their direct report when they enable functioning, but miss many opportunities to increase performance and engagement. Conversations become 'clunky' when there is a mismatch between what is going on in their heads and what is going on in the conversation. This mismatch will cause both parties to think they are not being heard, that they don't *get* each other, or that they can't help each other. They may start to doubt each other's motivation, capability or understanding. Perhaps they both start to doubt their own capability. You can see how quickly clunking conversations will lead to dissatisfaction, growing inauthenticity and stagnant behaviours.

Clash

Clashing conversations between a manager and a direct report are unfortunately relatively common. Perhaps this is caused by a lack of congruence on values, goals, or a difference in expectations of roles or tasks. Participants avoid or mishandle the 'real' conversations. Both individuals will start to label the issue within the other, and stop looking for solutions between themselves. 'Offline' conversations start to involve other people, sucking up time, profits and energy exponentially.

Clashing conversations undermine the quality of work and client service, as the emotions (e.g. anger, resentment, sadness or anxiety) take centre stage. The victim (to quote

Karpman's drama triangle (Karpman M.D., 1968)) will withdraw, say less, say yes, and start to fear more, hide more and do less. In clashing conversations, the opportunities for mutually beneficial growth are unlikely. A ripple effect wings its way out to other team members, other teams and clients; and, very quickly, the brand.

Cut

At times, conversations are completely cut. The opportunities to check engagement and adjust as necessary are absent. The direct report *may* grow of course, despite the breakdown in this area, particularly if they are driven to self-manage. But this is a large risk for the manager and business. The result is over time likely to be a poor performing and disengaged team member, who starts to lose sight of the relevance of their role to their own goals. We will also most certainly lose access to the direct report's knowledge and experience.

Where are *your* growth conversations currently with your direct reports? How can you get yourself higher up that ladder more often? When are you better than at other times, and with whom? Can you see that if you are pulling yourself into being in the top right quadrant of people management, to be a contributor, then you will need to have more clicking conversations?

On the following page is a table that shows us the impact of the different types of conversations we can have. When we have a clicking conversation, we create opportunities for growth and engagement. With a clunking conversation, we miss opportunities and engagement is vulnerable. Clashing conversations destroy opportunities for growth in people and connection and, therefore, efficiency and profit. This becomes worse if the conversations start to be cut.

Conversations	Potential to contribute to growth	Engagement	
Click	Exponential	Energised	$$$
Clunk	Limited	Vulnerable	$
Clash	Unlikely	Uninvolved	-$
Cut	Absent	Gone	-$$$

Table 1: Conversations create growth

Qualities of a clicking conversation

We are all busy. Our to-do list is never ending, and I bet you can't remember the last time you didn't have something pressing on your mind. It is easy for us to dismiss or let go of the immediate need to contribute to other people's growth. But we don't want to slip into the 'lazy' or the 'limp' state of people management. Growth conversations are ongoing. We must focus on creating clicking conversations with a regular, satisfying and smooth consistency...click, click, click. Keep thinking of that office toy...

Consistency is the key to making someone feel you are focused on them. This is an essential part of the trust and safety variables we will discuss. Consistency and frequency are not only best practice when maximising growth opportunities for the individual, but for the business, too. Consistency is not enough. There are also some key skills and qualities that you will need to master if you are to increase the effectiveness of your clicking conversations.

Empathy

One of the most helpful *and* unhelpful elements of effective conversations is empathy. We use empathy to put us in the other person's position and understand things from their point of view. This is something I encourage. If you don't find this easy—please practice...a lot. Think of it as a muscle that can be strengthened or a skill that can grow. Use the themes of this book to enable your own growth.

Helpful questions to grow your empathy

How would I feel if this were me? When have I chosen a similar response? What would have to happen in my world for me to make the same choices/have the same emotions? If this was someone I loved, what would I think about their situation? Can I imagine having had the life/week they have had, and what I would be feeling/thinking? What are they seeing, thinking, feeling, doing?

So, when could it be unhelpful for you to imagine it from their point of view? Well, put simply, they are not you. You do not have the same background as the person you are trying to help grow; you don't have their biases in thinking (you will have your own); you don't have their relationships, experiences or health. There are all sorts of identified biases that make your perceptions different. For example, when we find it hard to change ourselves, we are quick to blame situational factors—external things that got in our way. But, when we look at others, we are more likely to think that their change didn't happen because of something intrinsic to their style, personality or even capability.

When someone doesn't change even though we think it would lead to positive outcomes, it is exasperating. But we would do well to remind ourselves that we are looking at it through our own eyes, and although clear to us there is obviously some block for them. The things that help *them* are not the same as those that would promote growth for *you*. We need to think about standing *above our empathy* so we can assess its accuracy/bias and its helpfulness.

Patience

The time it takes for change to occur is difficult to predict. When someone has been behaving in one way, perhaps all their life, to switch is hard. Sometimes growth happens very quickly; you afford someone the opportunity to do something that stretches them and they rise to the challenge, exceed, and by default, grow. Other times you might need to lower your expectations of speed of growth, for your own sanity. Remember how hard it is to change.

Trust

Jean Valjean, the angry ex-convict in *Les Miserables* met Bishop Bienvenu at the beginning of the story. The Bishop trusts him to stay the night. Jean Valjean breaks that trust by stealing some precious silver goblets and is caught the next day. The Bishop makes a second and even larger expression of trust by telling the police he gifted the silver to Jean. In a third demonstration of trust, the Bishop gives him more treasure—a pair of silver candlesticks. He trusts Jean Valjean to use the silver to become an honest man.

Trust is future-based. It is a move based on the hope for a better future. Someone needs to demonstrate trust first—whether it be in a new relationship, or after a break in trust. But imagine if you demonstrated trust first, in the hope of a better future and they don't reciprocate; does it mean you stop trusting them, stop believing that a better future is possible with this person? Or do you demonstrate trust a second time? How many demonstrations of trust are you willing to make without reciprocation?

Many variables will determine your answer, including your history, your need, the perceived risk, your pride. You will have a bias towards 'to trust or not to trust', a bias in your hope for a better future. Which way does your bias lead you?

I argue that as the people manager you should take responsibility for creating greater trust if you want to have the most powerful impact on growth (yours and theirs). I think lack of trust is key to understanding so many missed opportunities for growth and engagement, so many clunky or clashing conversations, and so many limp and lazy people management patterns. Trust needs to be measured constantly. When it is out of balance, there is a need to address it. This precedes any development conversation, any growth conversation, any business development. There is no room for pride if you want to increase trust. You will be the one taking the risk (and sometimes several times), but good growth conversations require trust. If someone doesn't trust you, the chances are you won't be able to have an authentic conversation about growth. The conversation that you are having face-to-face, will be much quieter than the one you are each having in your own heads...clunk, clunk, clunk.

If your direct report breaks trust, it is an opportunity to have a clicking conversation; it is tough and it is not to be avoided. The following chapters will help you focus on growth as an outcome.

Warmth

Warmth is fast becoming the thing that separates the contributing people managers from those who are relying on hierarchy to lead. We all crave warmth, even those of us who deny it. It is a human (animal) instinct and is synonymous with care. Do you convey warmth? What would your direct reports say?

One of the simplest ways to show warmth is to smile. Do it in front of the mirror. If warmth isn't easily expressed in your physicality, you will be missing a contributing driver of growth. Without perceived warmth, you won't be providing the safe environment necessary for them to feel that you can 'hold' or add to their growth. Developing your capacity to feel and show warmth is critical. I was recently in a meeting where the leader stood up, banged his fist on the table, and shouted at the top of his voice, with no sense of irony 'I don't know why you are all so scared of me'. Remember that your tone and your non-verbals will be overriding your verbals, so don't forget to focus on warmth.

Appropriate environment

Your environment, and your current state also drive your capability, comfort and your biases in any given conversation. You may need to alter your environment to make a conversation more effective. You can change your environment to make the clicking conversation more effective. It may be, for example, that a café is more appropriate than a formal meeting room. Assess and then use the environment (or time) to aid your conversation, not work against it. For example, talking to your direct report about errors in a piece of work, as you are both walking into his client presentation, is probably not great timing. Likewise, if a person catches you in the corridor and tells you how hard they are finding managing their workload, you may want to reposition.

Sometimes you need to think about simple things like your seating position during the conversation. Probing someone while sitting opposite them with a table between you is a bit like a scene from an interrogation movie. We want to make them feel comfortable, not defensive. Sitting at 90 degrees will reduce the likelihood of inducing a threat response. A walk around the block is even more 'safe'. This enables us to avoid looking at each other, making us feel more comfortable and gives us the safety required to delve a little deeper or work through tougher emotions. Have you ever noticed that the most in-depth conversations happen when you are on long car journeys? Eyes forward is the least confrontational, the safest and the least inhibiting for conversations of depth in a professional setting.

Other things that can strengthen safety include giving boundaries of time, place or purpose. Making the person feel comfortable by ensuring they understand the context on which to frame the conversation. For example, asking someone 'How do you think you are going here?' as an opening to a growth conversation without setting the boundaries or purpose of the chat, could be misperceived. They might think that you are using it as a lead-in to talk about poor performance, and their physical and emotional reactions will prohibit their thinking and impact their response. They are more likely to try to guess what it is that you want them to say, than to be able to reflect carefully and contribute to the conversation authentically. By not setting the boundaries, inadvertently the scope of the opportunity for growth in that conversation has been reduced. You may even start an unnecessary cycle of behaviour where they act defensively and you, confused, react ... clunk, clash, cut.

True hearing

How irritating is it when you are telling someone something, and they assume the conclusion and respond accordingly before you have explained yourself—only they've assumed wrongly. It means we have to correct them and/or we lower the value we perceive in that conversation, perhaps in that person. This is the sort of clunking conversation that starts to alter what we share in the future.

Good growth conversations are built on listening, not assuming. Therefore, your role as a listener is to remember that the conversation is an opportunity to learn. Remain curious, and not force them into your own biases. But, I think it's more than listening—we need to *hear*. This difference, which some might view as semantics, is essential in my world. It helps remind me that there is more to do than just listen; it is much more oriented towards growth. Some people learn the tactics associated with good listening, such as staying silent or interjecting 'umms' and 'ahhs', or even pausing and summarising. Yes, these are great skills, but we must focus on the act of being open and hearing, more than simply listening.

We hear (as opposed to listen) by focusing on the whole message. Not just the verbals used right now, but the non-verbals, the patterns, the position of the message within its environment or this person's experiences. Wide, wide, wide. We must broaden our perspective so that we give ourselves the best chance to understand how to help others in a good growth conversation. Keeping wide and hearing are ways of being; it is more than a set of processes.

In addition to your own capability to hear, you need to reflect on how the other person is hearing what *you* are saying. There might be a misperception between the message you think you are giving and what the other person is hearing. A common way to counteract this miscommunication is by asking them to repeat what you just said. If they can repeat it well, you might think you have done your job. But listening, and even repeating, is not the same as hearing, and content is not the same as a message.

The only way you will determine if your message has been received is by checking the behaviour you were trying to influence. Has their behaviour changed? No? Then it is your responsibility as a contributing people manager to pick up the growth conversation again and try a different conversational theme, a different way of delivering that message, or perhaps use a different message.

Helpful questions to grow hearing skills

Is this verbal message congruent with other information I have? How can I check that I understand this completely? How can I further my understanding of this? Is my immediate understanding correct? Can I ask a question that enables them to refute what I think? Have I given them enough time to reflect? Have I given them enough 'room' to create the message?

Questions and probing

Asking questions is a key component of the clicking conversation. It demonstrates our curiosity to understand, and our drive to serve.

Questions like what, why, when, how and where, will of course reveal more and help you dive deeper. Open questions or statements such as 'tell me more' or 'could you give me an example?' will also help reveal more. Asking the same question several times will also encourage more content and reflection. Repeatedly asking 'why' after an answer is given is called the 'downward arrow' technique, specifically because it helps the other person to go deeper with each response. It will help you go quite deep very quickly, so use this technique with caution. You will end up at people's values and core sense of self if you keep going with asking 'why'; it can be very revealing, but can also be perceived in a workplace as inappropriate.

If we want to probe in any given conversation, we need to provide a trusted space so they can feel safe enough to reveal a bit more. This requires validation, appropriate energy and visible commitment to the person's wellbeing. The art of good conversations for growth (in fact good conversations for many things) comes down to the balance of probing. This skill set separates those who are good at growth conversations and those who are not.

The premise for probing is that you enable growth by either the individual joining the dots, or revealing something that enables you both to create a solution previously unplanned. By revealing the things that will slow down or stagnate growth, we have an opportunity to activate growth. From a more transparent position, our conversations are more authentic, and more opportunities are presented.

I think a good conversation has the ability to probe a little to discover any blocks that are preventing growth. However, I want to enable the person to feel as safe as possible, give them as much choice to share or not share. I would hate to feel like I have 'tricked' a person into telling me more about what is beneath the surface, so coming up to the surface for light relief by talking about something unrelated or something very 'light' will enable the person to assess for themselves whether they are comfortable. As an example, I may dip down with a probing question (or series of questions), and follow up with a surface comment or by using light humour to enable them to 'retreat' to safety. Then later, I might dip down again and take it deeper into a dive, in order to probe enough to increase my knowledge. Remember that you both only need to dip as far as is relevant to the conversation. This is not therapy. Stay relevant to the work or the growth, or else you will increase distrust.

Going under the surface must be done with care and permission. Sometimes it can come across as 'going too deep', putting you in control too much, and because of that the other person will withdraw and try to pull you back up to the surface conversation. Remember, you may be dealing with long-standing behaviours here, expectations of relationships and cultural norms. If people feel exposed they will be defensive in future conversations, wanting to stay at the surface and stubbornly refusing to go deeper. You may be familiar with that sense when you speak with someone who has been asked one too many questions for their liking. Asking if it is OK to ask a few more questions gives the other person permission to say 'no'. However, remember the power imbalance in the relationship. As the most 'powerful' person hierarchically, you will also need to keep an eye out for anything that displays you haven't got permission to discuss the probing questions.

Get to know your preference for depth, and whether it shifts around people and circumstances. Notice if you ascend because it is a way to enable safety, or because dipping or diving makes you feel uncomfortable. Start to be deliberate with your conversational depth and see if by stretching your skill, you enable more clicking growth conversations.

Examples of dips

How are you doing? What did you think of X? What did you make of Y? Was it a good outcome? Would you need something different next time? Did it make sense to you?

Examples of dives

Why? How does that relate to X? What did it mean to you? How did it feel? In what way?

Questions and probing are skills to be practiced, and ideally with someone who can help you comprehend your skill level and give you information on how it feels. Keeping the premise of service as your guiding principle of people management will help keep you on track. If you know that sometimes your actions are misunderstood, take some of your own opportunities for growth by focusing on your conversational capability.

Synthesising

Towards the end of a conversation, it may be helpful to synthesise the key information discussed. In other words, pull together in a closure summary the context, the meaning extracted and the actions discussed. This not only gives a chance for both parties to check their understanding, but it builds on the need for information to be organised effectively to increase the likelihood of remembering it and using it as a platform for the future clicking conversations. In this synthesising stage, keep curiosity as your guide, rather than confirmation. Building the skill of effective synthesis is one of the ways you can stretch the value of your conversations. Recording yourself to see how conversations end is a good way to plot your skill development.

How does growth happen?

Sometimes we go through an event (positive or negative) and our internal (thoughts and feelings) and external (behaviour) being changes. Perhaps you discover something about yourself, your life or your relationships or you are given an opportunity to do something you have never done, or are successful in a way you hadn't thought possible. Perhaps you learn a new skill, practise a new behaviour, or understand something for the first time. Perhaps by seeing a piece of art, a wonder of nature, architecture or culture, you experience an emotion that is so extreme that you cannot 'unfeel' it. It may be something as simple as trying a new cuisine or reading something that opens you up to appreciating a new culture, and it transforms your life forever by changing your behaviours. It may be that a new relationship, a new experience or a new role alters your perspective. It may be a large event or a small event, a large learning or a small one. It may be passive in that it finds us, or active in that we strive for it.

For active growth to happen, there are three things that need to be present.

1. **Inspiration:** To install new behaviours or learn new things, we need to counteract our old behaviours *and* we need to face the pain of growth. This will be true whether we are talking about a major growth point such as growing in confidence, or whether we are talking about a minor growth like completing a time sheet at the end of each day. In order to go through the adaption to a new behaviour we must want to do it, we need the pull of a goal, a goal that inspires us. Without inspiration, really, why would we bother? The more important the goal is perceived, the more likely we are to persist. Our job as a manager might be to strengthen the inspiration or to link the current task and their bigger purpose.

2. **Comprehension:** We need to understand our current situation, our desired situation, and have some ideas on what is needed to bridge the two. We also need an understanding of what might get in our way both inside our heads and outside in reality. As a contributing manager we must strive to aid this comprehension, to provide clarity of where they are now, where they are going, and what might get in their way.

3. **Perspiration:** Growth is hard and requires hard graft and sweat! Most of us want to be different, but do we want to go through the change required to get us there? Just look at the desire for weight loss. The tasks are not that difficult: eat less, do more. The hard bit is making the consistent behavioural choices that move us closer towards our goal. Growth usually involves some sort of risk, and doing new things. A certain level of dedication and grit (as Angela Duckworth (2016) discusses in her book of the same title) is needed. As a contributing manager, our role becomes to support this perspiration. In what way can we make it easier, more likely and less painful?

At work, we hope that we enable passive and active growth of our colleagues. Growth happens with longevity, experience and new challenges. We also try to influence growth in our colleagues through learning and development programs (either external or internal) whether that is through experience, training or ongoing support, coaching, mentoring and new opportunities. This book is not to qualify the value of all these types of learning or to suggest one over the other. It is to focus on the one aspect that I believe underpins the extent to which you as a people manager can maximise these opportunities: the quality of your conversations.

Figure 3 outlines the contributing people manager's growth model. If you want to propel your direct reports engagement and performance in every conversation you have, use clicking conversations to support inspiration, comprehension and perspiration. If you take just one thing from this book, it is this model. Your own performance and personal satisfaction, their performance and their engagement, rely on this model.

Ask yourself why should they do this task/grow? What needs to be done? And how might they do it? Conversations are your key to driving growth for your colleagues. The following three chapters explore these triggers in more detail to ensure that you make growth happen.

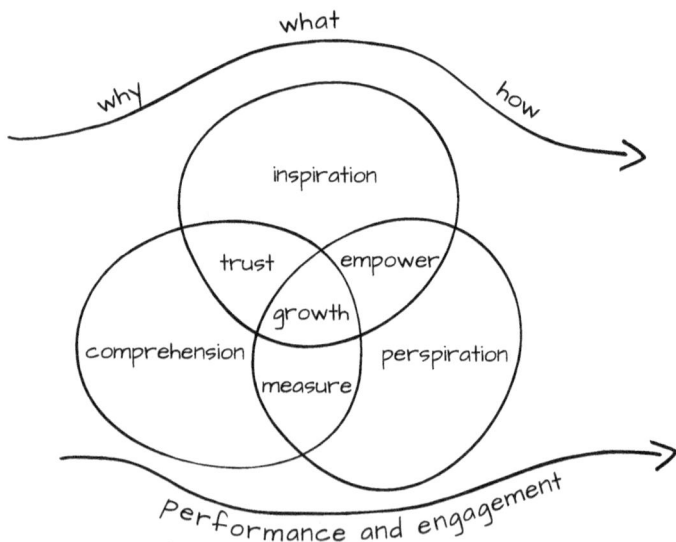

Figure 3: The model of growth conversations

THREE

Propel growth through inspiration

One of my specialised roles as a clinical psychologist was to improve the quality of life for patients who had been labelled 'difficult to treat'. Sometimes these individuals self-harmed or had a history of repeated suicide attempts; some found themselves repeatedly in patterns of unhelpful behaviours or abusive relationships. Before entering my office, these patients had already been treated with several other therapies; they had long histories with mood difficulties (depression and anxiety related) and/or behavioural problems (violence to self or others, or substance abuse). People often started their therapy with no faith that life would be any different as a consequence of the treatment.

People were often described in their referral as having low motivation to change. But to me, *low motivation* just meant we hadn't found the motivation yet. Motivation is not a characteristic; it is a state derived from a certain situation.

Let's assume that if people have found their way into a position where they are managed by you, they will be bringing a fair amount of their own inspiration. Simon Sinek (2013) talks about our *big why,* and famously said, 'Those who truly lead are able to create a following of people who act not because they were swayed, but because they were inspired'. You will need to keep inspiring them, you need to take responsibility to help them grow so they stay committed, and so you can rely on them for growth. There are many ways to help inspire your colleagues, including surrounding them with role models of excellence, providing great opportunities to work with certain clients within certain industries, or to learn new skills. In any growth conversation, the task for us as people managers is to enable motivation and find inspiration that will make the difference.

Inspiration is the process of being stimulated to do or feel something. If someone is inspired to do something, they are more likely to do it. For example, if Mel is inspired to check the details of her work so she builds her reputation with her clients, she will be more likely to fight against the pain associated with the task of triple-checking her work. However, if she doesn't have a why, a reason or inspiration to do this, she will find it hard to change the behavioural habit of rushing through her work. Why would anyone want to go through the hard work of change when they can't see why they should?

Inspiration is like a magnet pulling us towards a future. When we focus on the point, the why, we move forward with momentum. Inspiration might be something with a community focus, such as happiness of humans, or have a more individual family base such as being able to provide choices for your family. It may be about wanting quality of life, or more money or time. It may be more personal, like building one's confidence, creating a simpler life or gaining a sense of achievement. We need big aspirations to drive us, and we need little ones to motivate us daily. If your direct reports cannot see how their daily tasks are related to their big 'why', opportunities for clunky conversations arise, and engagement and performance slip.

As a contributing people manager, it is your role to grow their inspiration. Having clicking conversations around inspiration is essential to those who:

- do not see their current tasks as relevant to their goals
- do not see an attractive goal
- want to get to their goal faster
- don't know how to realise their aspirations
- don't have self-belief in their potential
- don't manage their tasks effectively for sustainability.

Inspiration parameters

Extrinsic vs intrinsic

Extrinsic motivation is when a tangible outcome is derived from the completion of the task—for example, money, title, rank. Intrinsic motivation is when a person is inspired to continue with a task with no external inducement—all benefits are internally derived, for example, satisfaction or pride. It's important to understand both parameters so that you have the full range of ways to help inspire your colleagues.

In the limp quadrant of people management, we can rely on the extrinsic motivations set by the organisational structure, the positive ones like bonuses, and the negative ones like written warnings. While conversations about extrinsic motivators may be inspiring, reliance on them is dangerous and can actually lead people to disengage. I think of these extrinsic motivations as the hygiene factors for inspiration. For example, without the pay matching expectations, there is a level of disengagement for the individual as they start to feel undervalued and overlooked. Sometimes the distraction is so great for both the individual and the decision makers, that the cost of all the meetings (offline and official) have a much larger price tag than the cost of giving someone a raise. Bonuses are great, and push individuals and teams to go for the goal they have set, and can in some ways lead to intrinsic rewards such as respect or pride. However, reliance on them can lead to a reduction of other reasons to do the task, and after a certain amount of time start to feel less motivating (e.g. annual bonuses are hard to tie to specific behaviours). In addition to the diminishing returns of extrinsic rewards, *not* being given a bonus could be perceived as a loss, and can run the risk of promoting unfavourable behaviours or start to feel 'empty' over time.

Gamification tools are proving incredibly helpful in driving behaviour by tapping into the inherent drivers of behaviour, and soon will probably be part of our working (and personal) life, driving our everyday behaviours. This involves making the tasks or behaviour change as rewarding as possible to the individual by giving points or tying it into a prize. Important elements in gaming include a sense of achievement, social sharing, engagement and competition. Recently, a client told me they had played a 'game' with two teams competing for a target in outbound calls. The achievements were recorded over a week and the winning team had 30 minutes each with a masseuse. In what ways can your conversations start to create more of a gaming attitude that might help the intrinsic motivation required? Perhaps scoring something, or keeping a tally of a behaviour might be helpful.

A people manager who contributes to growth will be having conversations about the underlying motivation to complete tasks or drive behaviour, both the intrinsic and the extrinsic ones. In Dan Pink's book *Drive* (Pink, 2011), he discusses the importance of purpose, autonomy and mastery. We have discussed purpose above, but just to reiterate, if the tasks or culture is off the key purpose and values of the direct report, we will not be inspiring them to grow. Autonomy is the desire to be self-directed. So herein lies the cost of micromanagement, or tasks that are unrelated to the individual's inspiration. By giving freedom of thought and task, your direct reports will be able to create and build something you can't see. Think about how you will use self-direction on a task to inspire someone's performance and engagement. Mastery is the ability to get better at something and subsequently feel good, feel satisfied. By enabling mastery over something, your direct report will value the work they do and the contribution they can make. As Dan says, 'When a person finds a job fulfilling, no further reward is necessary'.

Them-focused conversations

When helping someone become more inspired towards change, we must ensure it remains about *their* inspiration, not yours. A common bias in human thinking is that of mindreading, where we imagine what someone else is thinking. Often, we will mindread others' motivations by using our own as a guide. For example, you might think 'I want others to see me in a good light, so I assume Geoff wants that too. Therefore, I can tell Geoff that people will think better of him if he consults more with his colleagues'. However, before speaking to Geoff, it is important to know if he is motivated by others' opinions of him. It might be that he isn't, perhaps his primary motivation is in getting things done quickly, in which case focusing on the opinions of others won't be helpful to this growth area. The point is we don't know what inspires growth for each other. Use the following pointers for staying on theme-focused conversations

1. Reveal: Our key task, as a contributor of growth, is revelation of their inspiration, not presumption. By keeping curious, we will avoid clunky conversations fuelled by mismatches in inspiration and hidden blocks to behaviour change.

2. Don't judge: Once we reveal their inspiration, the next task for the contributing people manager is to withhold judgement. Judging will not help you stay curious, by default it will introduce the opportunities for clashing conversations.

3. Build: The third task of conversations that focus on inspiration is looking for links to build on this inspiration. Enable them to see that their potential is greater, or that their purpose is bigger. If someone wants to make a real difference, explore what this means for them: How do they feel they are going with that goal? How can you or the business support them with it?

4. Stay curious: The fourth, and most crucial, step is to enable their inspiration to change as they grow. Remain fluid in your expectations of what inspires them. Don't get caught out by thinking, 'but they told me that X was what motivated them, and now they are saying Y motivates them. What is going on?'. Keep stretching to *hear,* and do not assume that the conversation is over because you understand. Keep talking and exploring, and remember you are dealing with a human who is fluid, not an algorithm which is fixed.

The balance between aspiration and inspiration

Talking to your direct reports about their aspirations is important; it is part of the conversation around inspiration. Of course, big aspirations are very inspiring and can really drive bold and creative decisions. Tim Ferris (2007) says we need these wild goals to give us the freedom to create unmapped routes: why work 40-hour weeks, when you can do it all in 4 hours? But we must be careful that the aspiration is not too far removed from reality. A conversation with a graduate about aspirations to be a partner, or to have their own business one day, could become disengaging for them if they view this goal to be too far into the future. They will lose focus on the task at hand, think it too small or irrelevant. Through a clicking conversation, you will need to find some closer daily, monthly, quarterly steps to keep them inspired. Build that link between the now and the future.

One of the key factors that underlie change is the sense of achievement. Black and white, binary (can/can't) conversations can become more inspiring once we move towards shades of grey. Take where they are now and score it as 0, and give the end goal a title and a score of 10. Work out what 5 looks like, and then what 4 and 6 look like. Each 'one notch up' should not be too far out of reach from the one before. Inspiration becomes possible rather than out of reach. Your conversations can then be task- and behavioural-based around *what needs to happen to move you up one notch*. This will inspire them to reach forward for a more do-able task, giving a sense of achievement towards their bigger inspiration. This will make their efforts sustainable. This can be gamified as suggested earlier, or part of the tracking for mastery.

Techniques to successfully inspire

Motivational interviewing

Motivational interviewing is a conversation-based therapy born out of working with patients who have an addiction (Miller & Rollnick, 2012). The basic premise of this method is to make sure that if I am trying to help you grow,

I don't force you to adapt to my way of thinking about your behaviour. When I don't try to get you to think the same way as me, you don't have to defend your position. From that more open, non-judgemental space, you can consider what it is about your current position that makes you want to grow. This taps into the autonomy required for growth.

In the past, we would help people stop smoking by pointing out all the reasons why it was not good for their health. But this has limited impact. Now we know that we need to tap into their own reasons for wanting to stop smoking. So, it may not be the increased risk of cancer that helps them stop smoking, but the fact that their hair smells and people will notice the smell when they walk into a room. Motivational interviewing is a style of non-confrontational conversation that enables someone to explore their own inspiration for growth. They don't need to defend their behaviour, or talk about how hard it is to stop, how guilty they feel that they can't stop, or even why they can't stop even though they know they should. It opens them to think about their 'why', placing their own value on the growth.

For people managers who want to contribute to growth, Motivational Interviewing (MI) has a great role to play in your clicking conversations. By enabling a defence-free space, your direct report can explore their own cognitive dissonance.

Cognitive dissonance is the psychological stress one feels by holding two beliefs that contradict each other. For example, Mike might think, 'I know that the best way for me to grow is to delegate more of my work to my team' and he might also think, 'I can't take the risk of delegating work to my team because it could damage my growth'. These two contrasting beliefs represent the struggle Mike feels when trying to grow the skill of delegation. Rather than explaining to Mike all the reasons why you think delegation is good, a contributing people manager may try to explore (without judgement) the cognitive dissonance between his two contrasting thoughts. By increasing the discrepancy between the two, and exploring the differences, we help Mike see how either option contribute to his bigger inspiration (say for him it is his family's happiness). This may help him make a decision and take action.

Exploring dissonance not only enables an evaluation of the purpose or value of the thoughts, but it can highlight the explicit choices we have, and the internal or external damage of that tension. Increasing the cognitive dissonance that someone is experiencing, by asking them to give more detail on the two conflicting ideas, can often enable clarity around the most beneficial action. See if you can practice your MI conversations about any of the performance issues you are working on with your direct reports, and explore what happens. Your task is not to provide the solution as far as you can see it, but to reflect on what they are saying, letting *them* reflect on the key reason for activation.

You can explore using MI when you are asking your direct report to do something they don't want to do. There are times when we need to ask people to stretch or shift their focus to reflect the needs of the business. When the focus needs to shift because of *your* needs, you really need a two-way relationship. It is far easier to ask someone to do something for you when you have developed consistent and frequent conversations about them and their needs. Without that established pattern of communication, you run the risk of tangling the Newton's cradle and heading for a clunky or clashing conversation.

The following steps are useful during MI conversations.

1.	Validate their experience	*'Not being able to take the risk to delegate sounds hard'.*
2.	Clarify their perceptions of the pros and cons	*'So on the one hand you don't want to take the risk to delegate, but on the other you know it is the only way you will be able to grow, and maybe the only way your team will too'.*
3.	Encourage further self-exploration	*'What do you think of that? Will it ever be a lower risk or a risk you can tolerate?'.*
4.	Leave the door open for moving to preparation	*'When have you been able to risk delegating, and what happened? Who do you admire in this area, and how do they do it?'.*

Nudge, and nudge conversations

The psychological understanding of how and why people behave in a certain way has led to the adoption of behavioural science units in the world of health, politics and economics. A nudge is any way in which we alter the behaviour of someone or a group, by introducing or highlighting a choice. It is not about taking something bad away from an individual's choice set, but doing something which gives the alternative favourable option an advantage. An often-used example is replacing junk food with healthy food at eye level on a supermarket shelf. No cognitive or emotional growth is required from the individual, just a simple twist on the environment that makes it more likely that a healthy option is chosen.

If Molly wants to improve her time management skills you may have a conversation that looks for environmental nudges. For example, solutions such as using a colour chunking time in her calendar, or inserting a reminder in the calendar to start and end the day with a 10-minute review may be useful nudges that help growth. It takes the decision out of her procrastinating and enables her diary to tell her what to do. Nudges are everywhere; they are easy to find if you start having conversations around what would make doing the target behaviour easier, for example, 'how can we change something about your seat/table/view to make this more likely?'

Let's look at inspiring your whole team. If, for example, you want to encourage creative thinking, nudge this by sitting round a circular table rather than a rectangular one. This inspires more contribution and fights power imbalances. To further this, a simple conversational nudge might be to ask each person in a meeting to offer an alternative solution to a problem presented. This encourages creativity without doing any complex design thinking training. If it is repeated every meeting, very quickly people will adapt this more creative style to their thinking (if you keep judgement at bay). Remember the trust developed and the safety assured will determine the success of these nudges.

Stories

Stories form a large part of our conversations. But have you ever noticed how much? I challenge you to examine your conversations today and see how many stories you tell and you hear. Over time, we have used stories to evoke emotion, capture history and enable growth. Gabrielle Dolan (2017) talks about the business imperative of using stories to inspire. They have huge impact on the person hearing them and, therefore, can be used as an effective tool to influence inspiration. Storytelling—because you enjoy telling—is fine in some circumstances, but within growth conversations it should be used as a tool to create inspiration. Whether you use a story as a nudge, to role model, to normalise or to segue, stories are an important part of inspiring others. Noticing how much you are currently using them and how engaging they are to affect change could be a helpful start to understanding whether you need to grow in this area.

Sometimes stories can become so fixed in our heads that they start to become filters for our perception. They start to colour our thinking so much that we stop looking for new evidence, 'resting' on the 'truth' of the story. We start to change our conversations to seek confirmation of our existing beliefs. We must be careful not to believe stories so much that they restrict our curiosity or increase our judgements or expectations.

Stories can become 'truths' very quickly. For example, we can start to define how likely a person is to change. If you have labelled someone as *not being able to grow*, then of course you will stop inspiring them to grow. This self-fulfilling prophecy is well discussed in children's learning literature, but it is the same in adult learning. Beware of the stories around other people's (in)capacity to change, and use your conversations to spot false stories that might need adjusting.

Watch out for labels, even positive ones, as they will limit your potential to help people grow. When you hear labels or stories about your direct reports (even if it is by the person themselves), use it as an opportunity to stretch the potential by adding a phrase that locates the label in the past. For example, if someone describes themselves as indecisive, you can re-label that as 'so you've been indecisive in the past'. This moves it into a state, rather than a trait, conversation.

You can further this growth activation by asking 'so when are you decisive?' This stretches their definition of themselves as black and white. It shows them the truth, which is of course that we are grey. Growth is determined by the bandwidth in which we play. Don't contribute to those limits by using unhelpful stories to underlie your conversations.

A note of caution for you is to be careful how much you contribute to stories in the first place. It's not unusual for me to find people holding onto a belief of themselves that was created after a clashing conversation years ago. The story becomes set in their brain; they see themselves as X, and all their life they had collected evidence that this was so. They have not retained any conflicting stories because the first one was so powerfully held. Watch your conversations, and don't make a pattern out of an incident. Watch yourself converse and become aware of how these conversations will affect the inspiration and, therefore, the growth of those around you.

FOUR

Propel growth through comprehension

I'm always intrigued when someone knows more about me than I do. I would say nearly everyone in my life has looked at my face more than I have. They know how my face moves, what my face does, and perhaps what my face reveals about my thoughts more than I do. Scary! When it comes to my performance, I think this is also true. I don't think many people know my intention as well as I do, but they certainly know the impact more than me. If someone were to help me grow, I would expect and need them to help me comprehend what I can't see.

As a rule, we are not good at giving each other information about something we think the other person can't see. This may be as simple as telling someone they have spinach in their teeth or something less simple, that they are abrasive when talking to colleagues. In fact, we are so bad at it, that having training on difficult conversations is a mainstay in professional development, and one that I am frequently called on to deliver.

If we want to help people grow, it is essential to have a conversation about the things that are relevant to their performance, even if they are unaware of them. I often see a significant amount of talk taking place *about* a person, but not directly *to* the person. 'Offline' meetings take up time; other people are drawn into discussions, eating up their time too. There may be complaints about colleagues' behaviour or performance, wonderings about promotions or pay, and about the positives and negatives of different divisions. However, because these conversations are 'offline', they are less likely to lead to solutions, and more likely to be filtered by biased thinking. People, or even whole departments or teams, become siloed or excluded.

Often, we avoid providing information to others to avoid the pain associated with difficult conversations. We think it might hurt them if they knew the 'truth', or sometimes we are worried we will overstep the mark. Our empathy can lead us astray. We may believe that by avoiding giving someone feedback we are saving the other person from being hurt. Ultimately, this 'hiding' serves them badly. We are protecting our own feelings at the cost of their growth. They will be held back without knowing the reason.

But what if we didn't avoid conversations, and instead learnt how to use conversations for comprehension, while learning to tolerate the feelings associated with this? Our ability to help people grow would be maximised.

Helping your direct reports understand where their performance is now, and what they need to do to get to their goal is a critical role for you. Passive growth can happen, of course, but as a contributor you want to drive this growth through clicking conversations.

Whether it is technical or human skills comprehension that is needed, let's first take into consideration the different ways we can provide insight. We can 'coach' the insight, where we ask a series of questions that enable the individuals to come to the answer themselves, or we can 'give' the insight, by telling the subject the answer. Each of these methods is useful for different things, people or times. Are you comfortable with both?

The desire to 'give' the answer is driven by our impatience or our perceived lack of time. It can also be less frustrating for the subject. However, given what we know (and was seen in Chapter 3: Inspiration for Growth), we are much more likely to implement and maintain a solution we have derived ourselves. Being comfortable to create the space for the individual to explore the answers themselves is a great gift for your direct reports.

Coaching for comprehension

Often, all that is needed is the space to reflect and verbalise. Sometimes you relaying to your direct report what they are saying is helpful too. The very act of talking aloud enables the clarity needed for growth. These classic coaching skills will serve you well and ensure that you are not imposing your own solutions before the other has explored their own through autonomy.

Sometimes we can actively promote comprehension by asking Socratic questions.

Socratic questioning

Socrates, the classical Greek philosopher, was known for his questioning style. Socratic questioning is a style of question that aims to prompt evaluation of thinking. Rather than telling people what he thought the answer was, he asked questions, which were designed to prompt critical evaluation of the options.

This style of questioning enables open curious thinking rather than forcing an individual to state their case. Paul and Elder (2006) of the Centre for Critical Thinking classify the types of Socratic questions:

> Questions for clarification: Why do you say that? How does this relate to X? Would you consider talking to X before you did this again?

Questions to find assumptions: What were you assuming there? What could you assume there? How helpful is that assumption?

Questions on the reasons behind behaviours: Can you give an example of where that has been true? What do you think caused that to happen, and why?

Questions on their viewpoint: What would be an alternative? What is another way to look at it? Would you explain why that is necessary, and who benefits? Why is it best? How are X and Y similar? What would the counter argument suggest? What would someone else think?

Questions to highlight consequences: What generalisations can you make? What are the consequences of that assumption? How does X affect Y? How does this tie in with that previous conversation we have had?

Questions about the question: What was the point of the question I just asked? What does X mean? Do you think that was a helpful conversation, and why?

Tim has just completed a presentation. Here is a conversation he has with his manager Alice, to show you how Socratic questions increase his clarity.

Tim: I thought it went quite well. They seemed engaged.

Alice: Yes, I agree. I thought it went well. Do you want to think about any areas of growth?

Tim: Sure.

Alice: OK. So let's just think, on a scale of 0–10 where would you put yourself, where 10 is the best presenter you have ever seen, and 0 is the worst?

Tim: Probably around a 3.

Alice: Why do you think a 3?

Tim: I think they were listening and, I mean, how exciting can you be when you are presenting heavy numbers and tables of figures?

Alice: So what do you think a 4 would look like?

Tim: Probably a bit more energetic, you know, a bit more engaging.

Alice: Ok. So how could you do that, bearing in mind what you said about the content?

Tim: Yeah, that's the hard bit really, making the data presentation interesting. They need to see the detail but it makes it pretty boring. I need them to understand the detail, so I need to tell them.

Alice: Mmm.

(silence)

Tim: I guess having fewer slides to go through would be better, so it wasn't so heavy. But how do you do that and still give them the detail?

Alice: So, by cutting down the slide deck you wouldn't be able to give them the detail they got today?

Tim: Yeah, although they probably didn't get the detail today because it's too heavy. They sort of tune out a bit. I reckon because it's hard to hear, but I need to give it to them. Double bind!

Alice: What could you do differently that would enable them to get the detail but get that energy up a bit?

Tim: Don't know. (Pause) I think they wouldn't understand it if I left out too much detail.

Alice: What do you think presenters that are a 10 do?

Tim: Spend a lot of time working out interesting ways to present it, like infographics or something, but maybe they have other people to do that – like an infographics team.

Alice: What have you seen that ticks that box? Are there any people at work or out of work that you can learn from?

Tim: I guess I am comparing myself to ones I've seen on YouTube and TED Talks.

Alice: Mmm.

Tim: I guess I should be thinking more about the way Mary, at work, does it. She's engaging but still manages to give the details if they want them. She has fewer slides and a bit more swagger.

(Pause)

Alice: What makes you a 3 and not a 0?

Tim: Not a 0? Because I get up. I stand up. I want to help them, and I understand my stuff and what we've done. They like me...I think.

Alice: What do you need to do to get to a 4?

Tim: I think I'll speak to Mary and see if I can pick up some tricks. I think, actually, just cutting down the slide deck and being smarter about the slides might help. They can always see the detail in the full report if they need, or if they ask I can tell them – that way it's more conversational anyway, which is easier.

Alice: Great plan. OK. What will stop you activating this plan?

Tim: Nothing.

Meta-awareness

Meta-awareness is the capacity to rise above oneself in order to look down on what is being done, and what is not being done. Distancing ourselves from our own thoughts and behaviours means we can start to observe them dispassionately, like an inspector would evaluate a suspect. From that position, it is easier to be less biased, and potentially less emotionally blocked.

Much of therapy focuses on developing meta-awareness as a tool for growth. The therapist is trying to help the patient increase their meta-awareness of their current state, and the gap between this and their future state. In essence, when developing someone's meta-awareness you want to be modelling, out loud, a conversation that at a later point they will have in their own head. As a therapist, the most rewarding end to an intervention is, 'I don't need you to continue to help me grow'. At this point, a patient's meta-awareness is so strong it feeds their self-empowerment and they know they have the skills to continue. As the saying goes, *give a man a fish and you feed him for a day. Teach him how to fish and you feed him for a lifetime—Lao Tzu.*

Use Socratic questions to start building meta-awareness for your direct reports. Imagine how helpful it will be for your direct reports to say (whether to you, or in their own head), 'Oh, there's that thought again' or 'I wonder why I thought that?' or 'Because I thought X, I did Y'. One of the implications of building meta-awareness successfully is that the person starts to develop a self-efficacy about their thinking and their reactions.

Patience and silence

When we coach (as opposed to direct) our direct reports towards comprehension, extra skills are required from us. We must be able to tolerate the other person's brain figuring something out. We are trying not to give them the answer, but let them draw their own conclusions through our questioning. It is in the silence after you ask a question that the hard work is done in their head, they get to join the dots or discover new ones. If you can stretch the silence longer after a question, you will see the magic play out. I am comfortable with silence. I often use it, but I know others find it hard. If you are not comfortable with silence, remember that their head will be busy. To them, the silence is not silence, but a whirring brain full of sentences and ideas. Remember, the gift of serving them through being a contributing people manager doesn't mean that you rescue them from the struggle of growth. Don't jump in and rescue their struggle simply because you can't wait.

Telling for comprehension

You can provide growth opportunities to your direct report by bringing them new information or giving them access to new information. This could be technical (e.g. new regulations or a new process or software) or personal (how to build trust with a client). You will need to spend time thinking about how someone is going to learn their new skill, and finding appropriate action.

Perhaps you will be the best person to model something, or train them in a process, procedure or human skill and talk them through the underlying skills that you are using. Rather than thinking of this as something that will slow you down, appreciate the connection opportunities that it gives you. Also, there is often huge personal benefit to teaching someone something; you see things from a different angle. Sometimes you will want to involve someone else, a coach or a trainer specific to their needs. You may also identify a need for a suite of learning through a course or mentoring process.

Another way to increase someone's comprehension and thereby contribute to their growth is by giving them some information about their performance. This could be about their current behaviour or about the behaviours or outcomes they might demonstrate next in order to reach their goal. Sources for this information come from their observations, your observations, others' observations, or the consequences of their actions.

What do you know about your direct report that you are choosing not to share, and do you know why you are doing that? Is it because you are trying to avoid a difficult conversation, or for a more valid reason relating to the usefulness of the conversation?

Not giving people the feedback that would enable their progress is the equivalent of leaving them in a dark room with the lights off, and expecting them to figure out an escape route. It doesn't take long for this to be a cultural theme for a workplace, and the knock-on effect of this is people walking around in the dark hurting each other as they collide.

I think we need to reframe feedback. We must stop seeing feedback as an end point. In fact, I passionately hate the word feedback, as it implies that it is one direction, backwards. To me, there is the opportunity to feed-growth through conversations that increase someone's comprehension of where they are and where they want to go. That sounds nice, don't you think? Perhaps if we all saw the provision of new information as part of the growth process, we would be able to tolerate it more, be less defensive or dismissive and learn from it more quickly. Perhaps if growth conversations were clicking away all over the place, increasing our comprehension would be seen as helpful, as opposed to what I see as the norm - fear in the face of feedback.

When I get called on to do workshops on difficult conversations, I quickly reframe it as Conversations that Create Growth. And yes, while I agree they may be difficult conversations, I want people to appreciate that the point of upskilling leaders in these conversations is not to make the conversations less difficult, but rather to enable the growth of their direct reports, their clients and their business. This shift in semantics puts the focus in the right place. The point is *feeding growth,* not feeding back. Providing new information to your direct report is part of the process, and when we understand how people grow (inspiration, comprehension, perspiration), we can see how important a task it becomes. We must take responsibility for this part of our role; we must get better at having clicking conversations around providing new information to our direct reports.

Once the focus is growth, the emotions change. There is a purpose to this difficult conversation, a point. Yes, there are skills involved in having these conversations and these can be learnt and practiced. Difficult conversations are difficult, but that doesn't mean they shouldn't happen. However, it does seem that we are poor at giving this information. Some 60% of employees have not been given useful feedback in the past six months, even though 62% of leaders rated themselves as highly effective at giving honest, straightforward feedback (OnDemand, 2013).

How much damage are you doing by not increasing the comprehension of your direct reports?

Preparation for thinking about conversations that may be difficult:

- What are you going to be talking about, and why? Is it an incident or effect? Is it role-critical?

- What is the ideal outcome of this conversation?

- When and where is this conversation best had?

- What behaviours might be worth tracking as a consequence of this conversation?

- How can you contribute to the 'growth' moving forward?

- See the information within the context of the building blocks of growth (inspiration, comprehension and perspiration).

All the points discussed in relation to 'good clicking conversations' (Chapter 2) become more important in these conversations. Empathy, patience, trust, warmth, appropriate environment, true hearing, questioning and synthesising are crucial. Providing information clearly and simply, with as little as possible of your own emotional baggage; will make for a better conversation. If you have been having conversations consistently and frequently, it should not be too hard to do. And in any case, this is about them, not you. The hard bit is doing it in a way that doesn't derail them, but leads them towards inspiration.

Measure progress for clarity

You can provide useful new information on a direct report's growth by tracking the target behaviour. Without tracking achievements, it is harder for them to feel progress. Feeling as if no progress is happening can be extremely disheartening for both you and your direct report. Humans need to see progress to make growth sustainable; it is inherently motivating and through all sorts of chemical reactions creates positive emotions—like pride. If you train for a marathon, you would use tracking to keep you motivated. You would set yourself targets and you would strive to achieve them. You might even write them down somewhere to hold yourself accountable and keep you motivated. When working with your direct reports on their growth, make sure you enable conversations that create growth by measuring behavioural change, attempts towards behavioural change and/or their feelings.

Measuring progress is key and should be linked to observable behaviours or 'their feelings'. Completing a presentation may be an indicator of experience but it is not an indicator of performance or growth. Something that would be worthy of measuring is outlined in the example earlier: does Tim feel he moves to a 4? This measure enables and encourages more growth for Tim. It may also be that you measure observable behaviour and enlist the help of someone in the audience (or yourself) to measure certain elements of the presentation, or for Tim to measure himself in a video replay.

You can use measurements in your conversations to discover why and where their behaviour shifts, and why and where it doesn't. Remember that you want to install meta-awareness, their sense of achievement and their sense of self-empowerment, so tracking success is crucial. It is all too easy for them to dismiss their growth as 'normal', or what anyone would do, or even forget that they had ever not known or behaved in this new way. It is up to you to track these things in an unbiased way and build on their clarity.

It may be that you map out progress visually: a simple tick sheet, flow chart, or a review of the 0–10 of their goal progress. You can help people break down the stages. You could also encourage your direct report to keep notes themselves. This can be numerical, like collecting the number of times they spoke in a meeting, made proactive decisions, took a lunch break, the number of times they were interrupted in a meeting, or stayed at work beyond 6 pm. It can also be in narrative form, such as a professional development reflection journal. The important part of this measuring is to use your conversations to analyse the findings. This gives you a way to develop their comprehension and through curiosity (not judgement) keep the conversation clicking towards growth. If you feel that, for whatever reason, the trust has slipped, you will need to re-set this first so this monitoring doesn't become (or is perceived to become) critical.

The accountability of progress is a key way to maintain strong engagement and performance.

Blocks to comprehension

We all have blocks that prevent us maximising our own growth. Some are environmental, some are habit-driven and some are errors in our thinking. Understanding how to spot our blocks helps us comprehend what needs to shift.

Unhelpful thinking habits

Humans are biased thinkers. Predominant Western thinking assumes we are born as a blank state. The task of childhood is to section off the information we receive and put it in easy-to-understand boxes ready for us to make shortcuts in the future. We cannot possibly process all we experience, and so the ability to filter our information through the lens of our pre-thinking is very helpful. Except it isn't always.

Humans are biased; our thinking is less about the truth and more about our history, our perspective. We distort reality all the time. So, when you are having a conversation with someone about their growth, watch out for biases.

Below is a list of common thinking biases. When we have conversations with our direct reports, and if we are to help them grow, we need to pick up on biases—theirs and ours.

All-or-nothing thinking (also called black-and-white, polarised, or dichotomous thinking): You view a situation in only two categories instead of on a continuum.

Example: 'If I'm not a total success, I'm a failure.' 'He is wrong, I am right.' 'There is no in-between; it either is or it isn't.'

Catastrophising (also called fortune telling): You predict the future negatively, without considering other, more likely outcomes.

Example: 'He'll be so upset he won't be able to function at all.' 'She will collapse if I tell her what people are saying.' 'He is going to go crazy.'

Disqualifying or discounting the positive: You unreasonably tell yourself that positive experiences, deeds, or qualities do not count.

Example: 'I did that project well, but that doesn't mean I'm competent; I just got lucky.' 'He missed the quality expected because there was an error on the front page of the 40-page document.'

Emotional reasoning: You think something must be true because you 'feel' (actually believe) it so strongly, ignoring or discounting evidence to the contrary.
Example: 'I know I do a lot of things well at work, but I still feel like a failure.' 'He's a good guy, so it can't be his fault.'

Labelling: You put a fixed, global label on yourself or others without considering that the evidence might more reasonably lead to a less disastrous conclusion.
Examples: 'I'm a loser.' 'He's no good.' 'He's a busybody.' 'She is a complainer.' 'I am the leader.' 'He is lazy.'

Magnification/minimisation: When you evaluate yourself, another person, or a situation, you unreasonably magnify the negative and/or minimise the positive.
Examples: 'Getting neutral feedback proves how inadequate I am.' 'Getting good feedback doesn't mean I'm smart.' 'They are terrible at X and, therefore, unreliable.'

Mental filter (also called selective abstraction): You pay undue attention to one negative detail instead of seeing the whole picture.

Example: 'Because I got one piece of negative information at my review (which also contained several high ratings), it means I'm doing a lousy job.' 'The client said they wanted X, so they aren't happy with the service.'

Mindreading: You believe you know what others' motivations are, or what they are thinking, failing to consider other, more likely possibilities.
Example: 'He's thinking that I don't know the first thing about this project.'

Overgeneralisation (also called global thinking): You make a sweeping negative conclusion that goes far beyond the current situation.
Example: 'Because I felt uncomfortable at the meeting, I don't have what it takes to make strong relationships at work.' 'They did X wrong, and that means they are not capable.'

Personalisation: You believe others are behaving negatively because of you, without considering more plausible explanations for their behaviour.
Example: 'The meeting was boring because I was in it.' 'They failed at X and it is my fault, because I never showed them Y.'

'Should' and 'must' statements (also called imperatives): You have a precise, fixed idea of how you or others

should behave, and you overestimate how bad it is that these expectations are not met.

Example: 'It's terrible that I made a mistake.' 'That mistake was disastrous. I should never make a mistake.' 'There must not be any failings.'

Tunnel vision: You see only the negative aspects of a situation.

Example: 'My manager can't do anything right.' 'He's critical and insensitive, and lousy at managing.' 'There is no point trying to fix this.'

When having conversations with direct reports, keep a mental log of how often some of these thinking distortions occur, and what type. Sometimes the biases are one-offs, sometimes they are themes, sometimes they are helpful, sometimes they are unhelpful. It may, for example, be helpful for a sales person to think that they are the best sales person ever.

If you spot a pattern that isn't helpful though, you have the choice to increase their comprehension, to notice the influence it has on their thinking style and their behavioural choices. You may, for example, spot it and say, 'it seems like that thought comes up for you quite a lot' or 'I noticed you said something similar the other day' or 'is that always true?' By having a conversation like that you will enable your direct report to raise their consciousness around the habit and comprehend its relevance to their growth. If you wanted to take this further, you may also be able to move them into a conversation that highlights the alternative viewpoints that could aid their growth:

1. Is there any other way you/we could look at this?

2. What would someone else say as an alternative perspective?

3. How much evidence have you got that this thought is true?

4. Let's collect some facts here so we don't just use our own thoughts.

Unhelpful behaviour habits

Sometimes people get caught in behavioural habits that are not helpful. Increasing their comprehension of when they behave in an unhelpful way will increase their ability to do something different. It enables them to increase the space in which they make a decision, and turns their actions into a response not a reaction. For example, Lisa wants to grow in her influencing skills, but you have noticed she becomes defensive when challenged. By showing her how and when it happens, she gains clarity over her behavioural blocks. If we are trying to help Patrick increase his ability to go over and above client expectation, we might show him how using last year's report as a template for this year's presentation might limit how he is able to 'wow' the client. In conversation effectiveness training, I will often use a video camera to show people how their body and verbal language habits contribute to to their ability to influence.

Once the behaviour becomes noticeable to the individual, they have more scope to change. As Carl G Jung said, 'Until you make the unconscious conscious it will direct your life and you will call it fate'. Not knowing where their unhelpful behaviours block them is key to tripping up growth in your direct reports. You can increase their comprehension through clicking conversations, consequently maximising their opportunity to grow.

FIVE

Propel growth through perspiration

Hard work and the perspiration that comes with it are necessary for growth. Creating new habits and doing new things is always harder than staying the same. This is true even when the current situation is unpleasant or not ideal. How many people do you know who stay in a situation because it feels familiar, even though it is horrible: relationships that should be over, jobs that should be left, and self-sabotaging behaviours that need to be dropped. We are creatures of habit, and although the desire to be different is often experienced, the perspiration required to make it happen is hard to endure. It is difficult for our brains to figure out new things; hence, our drive to stay away from the unfamiliar.

Conscious change requires hard work. When working with a direct report on their growth areas, it is crucial to reflect on the perspiration required for change. Let's take, for example, the process of helping someone with perfectionist tendencies that slow down their efficiencies and increase their workload. If we want to help them grow, they will need to learn to tolerate imperfection; they may need to focus on the risk of delegation, the discipline of having to learn new uncomfortable habits, creating boundaries, learning how to tolerate the feeling that they could have done better, and so on.

This chapter is about the ways in which we can support people with the perspiration required for growth.

Beware of your expectations

When our focus is the growth of our direct reports, we must first consider our own assumptions about how easy or how hard it is for them to change. The self-fulfilling prophecy associated with leadership is demonstrated often. Having expectations of success and believing in people's ability may be really helpful to their growth. However, we must be cautious of believing in someone so much that we set them up with limited support. Likewise, believing that someone cannot change, or will not be able to shift due to rigid personality traits, means we are unlikely to give them the opportunity to do so. The balance of 'belief in' and 'support of' becomes a key feature of a great contributing people manager.

If we use ourselves as a guide and assume that because it is easy for us it will be easy for them, we may be wrong. Our ability to support this task or this person may be consequently blocked as we turn off our thinking about ways to help, set up, manage and measure their achievements. It could also lead to our disappointment, frustration or anger when the discussed task isn't completed. I mean, it's easy isn't it?! How will your direct report feel if you think this is an easy task, but they don't? It makes it more likely that they will say 'oh yes, I understand' or 'easy done!' when in fact they don't understand and they don't find it easy. This is how 'easy' errors are made at great cost—through assumptions made in clunky conversations that miss opportunities to enable growth through support.

We also create unnecessary problems when we make assumptions that the change or growth planned for our direct reports is harder than it actually is. If your direct report picks up that you think this is a hard task they are more likely to lose confidence in their ability to do a good job. Perhaps it takes the excitement away from the challenge and makes it ominous and scary, and here we are welcoming back the self-fulfilling prophecy. If we think the growth area is hard, or that the change required is uncomfortable for our direct report, we avoid trying to talk to the person about it. It is as if we don't want to burden them with it or we don't want to be the one to support them through it because they will probably fail; and how cruel is that? Perhaps we are even worried about our own failures in being able to help, or our own uncomfortableness with having to talk about it. We may layer on a whole load of unnecessary emotion. This is the very thing that underpins the reticence I see managers having in giving people accurate or timely feedback or feed-growth information.

What about our micro-managers, the ones who don't have trust in their direct reports, or can't let go? Not once in my whole career has anyone said much in support of the micro-manager. They close down autonomy, they limit growth through lack of exposure, and they increase insecurity and cautious behaviour (for both the manager and the direct report). This is support of perspiration gone too far. I see micro-management as a habit and one that can be shifted as most habits can, in the same way we are discussing in this book. Therefore, for those of you who are insightful enough to recognise you have this habit, you may need to think about how to increase your 'belief in' or test yourself with less 'support of' your direct reports, and see what happens.

Screening ourselves as the leader and trying to 'cleanse' the situation from our own stuff, will enable us to help our direct reports more. Keep focused on being curious, open and empathic to balance out your expectations. The only one who can define the task of change, and the perspiration required for that growth, is the person doing the change.

Stages of change

Prochaska and DiClimente (1984) presented a 'stages of change model' to explain the process for behavioural change in patients with addictions. It has since been replicated and supported as a model to understand most behavioural change. An individual doesn't go through these stages in a linear way, but rather it is a cycle that can help us understand the backwards and forwards continuous process of bringing about conscious change.

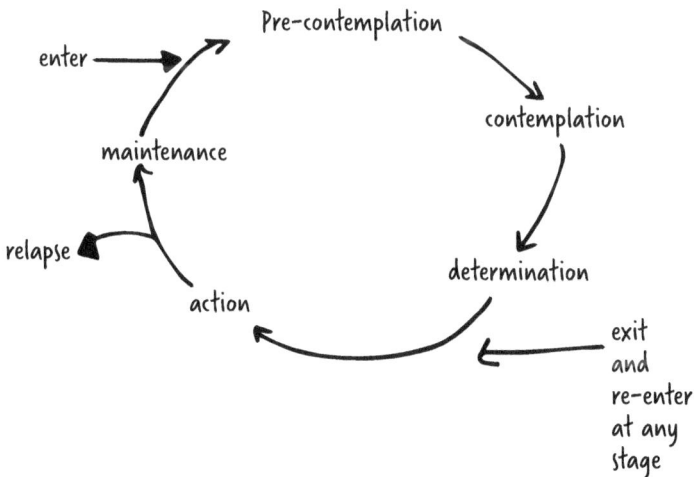

Figure 4: Stages of change model (Prochaska and DiClimente)

Precontemplation

At the first stage, the individual is unaware of the need to change, or is not intending to take any action. Four reasons for staying in this stage are reluctance, rebellion, resignation and rationalisation. If a person is at this stage, it will be important to help them see that there is a benefit to the growth. Sometimes this can be a consequence of providing feedback/feed-growth or gaining clarity (see Chapter 4).

Contemplation

The person recognises there is a need to change, and they start to evaluate the advantages and disadvantages of doing so. If your direct report is at this stage, it is important to have conversations around dissonance, as in Chapter 3.

Preparation

In preparation, the individual starts to take small steps towards the behavioural change. When someone is at this stage the tracking becomes relevant and prudent, as seen in Chapter 3.

Action

Here the person makes overt modifications to their behaviour either in a move away from a problem behaviour or towards a new behaviour. Conversations clarifying progress or accountability will be important.

Maintenance

There is a need to maintain this new behaviour in a variety of situations for it to be assimilated as a new behaviour. Tracking is important here of course, but so is reframing their progress within the context of self-empowerment.

Termination

Once at this stage there are no temptations to return to old behaviours. While this is a good news story, it also implies the need to introduce other areas of growth. Without growth, remember that people will start to feel stale and disengage, so if this is your direct report, make sure you are lining up the next challenge that they want to take on.

Relapse

Relapse is always a way someone can 'fall off' this cycle of change. At a point of relapse, the person feels the pull to their old behaviour. Once back on the cycle, a person can join any stage of the cycle. In a work context, the relapse could be something like a slip back to old behaviours or a loss of motivation to grow. Or perhaps a drawback to perfectionism in times of stress. The manager's task becomes to build comprehension, support perspiration and join the 'now' to the future inspiration so they can return to an active part of the cycle.

As a contributor to growth, it is important to remember that there is no normal amount of time associated with any of these stages, but they do occur in the order shown. Tuning into where your direct report is on any given change or growth point will give you guidance on what is needed from you, and how you can help. I think it is also a great reminder that what is needed changes over time. You can get stuck trying to persuade someone to move from pre-contemplation to contemplation when they are already there. This may feel unhelpful to them, and will start to lead to clunky conversations. You may wish to use the stages of change model as another way to prepare yourself for what is needed from you in any given conversation, and how you might be able to best support them. Ask yourself (or them) where they are at before you decide how you will support them.

Stages of support

There are many stages associated with helping people grow. If you are to help, and not hinder someone's growth, it is essential to be aware of these stages and know how to manage people along their journey.

The task of parenting can be split into two stages. The first is full of dependence when the child requires the parent in order to function and stay alive. The second is when the task of the parent is to pull back, to enable the child to become independent. For example, in reference to a child at a playground, you will often see a parent of a toddler hovering under the climbing frame, placing the child's feet and hands on the metal rungs to enable their progress up the frame. This is direct support and is required at the early stages of their growth as a climber. However, if this continues for longer than necessary it will start to disable the child's ability to learn. The indirect support starts when the parent decides to step back and take risks with their own feelings and the protection of the child. In this stage, they enable the toddler to wobble, perhaps even fall in order to get a sense of balance and danger, and to encourage their tenacity. Of course, we may kick some extra woodchip underneath them and restrict how high they go; we don't just walk away and cross our fingers. So the second stage is not hands off, rather it is a different stage of support.

The stages of growth of your direct reports are similar. Your first role in directing their growth is metaphorically placing their hands and feet in the right position and providing clear direction that keeps them safe. As they progress, your second role is to step back, to drive their self-empowerment and for both of you to become comfortable with the risk of a wobble or fall. Here, the stepping back safely is not turning your back and 'wishing' that growth in capability comes, but rather putting forms of accountability and tracking in place. You gauge how someone is doing by checking in with them or their metrics—supporting from a distance. One of your tasks as a contributor to growth is to keep practicing these stages of support so you are introducing new climbing frames at the right time, remembering that your direct reports need to feel challenged (but not too challenged), and they need to recognise that they are growing continuously.

Supporting failure

What about when people fail? We are humans, not widgets. People are fallible and will make mistakes. Our behaviour and support, at that point, will have wide-reaching consequences. Again, starting with you, what are your beliefs about failure? Do you believe it is a sign of weakness or a sign of growth? Do you believe it is the end, or simply a part of the process of change? Do you believe it is to be avoided or encouraged? This is, in essence, the discussion that has become part of our disruption and innovation cultural norm. It is important to realise that you will have your own thoughts about this in relation to people change. Do you tolerate people falling off the climbing frame? Of getting stuck at certain points, or of people needing the stage one parenting for longer than you want to? These are all questions that are posed in your direction as a manager who wants to contribute. People are not the same, will not require the same support as each other, or as you would. How you support failure will determine their growth.

Helping someone get up when they fall is essential to building future growth, not only with the current task but in unseen, future areas too. I was once working with a leader who responded to mistakes so severely that he started to inhibit people's creativity and risk-taking. Likewise, I am grateful to have worked with many leaders who use failure as an indication that the support level wasn't right, that some other system required change, or they had a fundamental belief that failure was essential to growth. In fact, I believe those leaders who have contributed most to my own growth have been those who have used the failures as an opportunity to dig deep into what we could do next. How can we use this information to learn and progress?

Anti-fragility is the concept first described by Nassim Taleb (2014) as gaining through adversity. He discusses the need for us to focus on the ability to grow from these events rather than just tolerate them and bounce back, as is common in resilience literature. When an adverse event happens (the loss of a contract or an error made), it is important for us to converse around this in relation to the lessons learnt, pushing our direct reports to view this as an opportunity to grow.

It may be that you feel you have supported previous failures well, but the failures continue. That your behaviour and management of their growth has been good, but their progress has not. In the growth model shown on page 24, you will see the join between support and clarification is measurement. Often it is this intersection that we use to plot the progress. If no progress is seen, then more measurement might be required, or measurement of different things. Having honest and open clicking conversations around these measures will enable you both to grow through the failure, and determine where to go next.

Supporting a growth mindset

An increasing amount of what we know about growth and our ability to adapt to the world around us is related to our mindset. How much do we let failure stop us persuading the hard work of change? Carol Dweck, Professor of Psychology at Stanford University, conducted a study where she gave a group of children a task that was out of their expected level, above their current skill set. She discovered two defined groups within the participants. The first she labelled as having a growth mindset: children who approached the task with enthusiasm and expectation that they would like to work out how to do it. The second group, who she labelled as having a fixed mindset, believed that they weren't going to be able to do it and didn't try, or gave up easily. Her book *Mindset* (2012) explains the importance of creating a growth mindset when helping people fulfil their potential.

So, perhaps good questions for you as a manager are, what are you doing to encourage a growth mindset in your direct reports? And, how fixed are you about your ability to have conversations that create that growth?

If you are like most people, you will respond with "sometimes s/he is, sometimes s/he's not"; "sometimes I am, sometimes I'm not". So the trick becomes, how to do you stretch your own fixed mindset when it appears, and how do you spot it in others? Dweck talks about the power of the phrase 'not yet' when helping shift someone from a fixed to a growth mindset. So now when your direct report says, "'I can't say no to clients", you may reply "you can't say no to clients, yet". It helps both of you set off on a path of growth even though it may require hard work.

Supporting implementation

Have conversations with your direct report about ways and systems that might make the growth behaviours easier. We know how hard change is. Consider the simple act of growing in fitness. Peter Cook, one of my favourite mentors, is a leading expert in implementation. He talks about setting up systems that make it less likely that he will 'relapse' on his desired behavioural change. For example, he sidesteps the desire to renege his exercise routine by arranging for the personal trainer to come to his house. Using this system, he doesn't have to deliberate and persuade himself to go to the gym; he doesn't give himself the range of 'outs' that might otherwise have been there. He minimises his decision fatigue.

I worked with a manager who wanted to help a person in their team become more independent, to ask fewer questions. Together they devised a strategy to meet every day at 4 pm for half an hour, for her to ask him questions and for him to answer. The direct repot stored her questions throughout the day, and this led to many new discoveries. She discovered that some of the questions answered themselves over time, she could find other people to ask questions of, and that way she developed other relationships and saved frustration in her relationship with her manager. She also started to prioritise questions, and over a few weeks they started 'gaming' the behaviour by seeing how many questions she could answer herself. It wasn't high risk for the manager as he was still keeping in touch daily, and the direct report knew that there would be opportunities for questions and answers every day. This strategy didn't have to be used for too long before a series of new habits were activated.

When you are helping support your direct reports grow into new behaviours, get together to think of ways you might be able to make it easier to sidestep the pull of the moment, the return to 'old behaviours'. What follows is a list of known ways in which we can influence people's behaviour, and you may both look to these as a way of thinking about supporting implementation of growth.

Social pressure

We commit to things when our behaviour is normed against others. In other words, when we think other people are behaving in a certain way we are more likely to behave that way too. This principle shapes our decisions and our commitments without us even knowing. So, for example, the utility bills that reference the average use in our street help us commit to lower energy use—we don't want to be the only one in the street using 2x the average. At work, an example might be showing a direct report how his cost ratios are different to his colleagues.

Public commitment

Committing to others is another way of ensuring action. For example, we can tell a partner or a friend, or even ask people to hold us accountable to the changes required for growth. If a growth target is discussed in front of others, there is public accountability to the behaviour change. If your direct report mentions in a team meeting that they are working on getting better at putting themselves forward for business development opportunities, they are more likely to make it happen. If a team publicly commits to its area of growth (e.g. attention to detail, time management, speed of decision-making, keeping to scope) members can support each other *and* provide social pressure.

Chunking

It is hard to commit to running a marathon without chunking the tasks. Similarly, if you have a longer timeframe, you might be wise to have weekly goals, which are a chunking of your time. Remember our discussion of performance reviews? This is where the ongoing conversations make more sense, in that they chunk down the time and turn end goals into achievable actions. As the old joke says: How do you eat an elephant? One bite at a time!

Supporting emotions of growth

There are many emotions associated with growth. There are the positive ones that go with a sense of achievement and pride. There are also the emotions that go along with watching others succeed, and a social sense of connection, safety and progress. These emotions build engagement, create meaning and strengthen commitment to what it is we are doing. When these feelings come up, it is important to notice them and hold them. I was recently with someone who had received wonderful information on her leadership from her team and yet she was unable to keep hold of it. She quickly wanted to dismiss it out of embarrassment, and a sense of not drawing attention to herself. But I insisted she stayed with the feeling for longer. It is all too easy to dismiss growth as inevitable or easy, once it has happened. For us to create more opportunities for growth we must revel in our achievements, take pride from our gains and celebrate our progress. If you want to contribute to the growth of your direct reports, look for opportunities to support their positive emotions.

There are also negative emotions that come with the process of change and growth. Rabbi Dr. Abraham Twerski uses the story of how a lobster grows to demonstrate how stress is a key component of growth. The soft and squishy lobster lives inside a rigid shell. As the lobster grows, the shell becomes uncomfortable and places pressure on the lobster. When the pressure gets too much it retreats to the safety of the rocks and hides while it sheds its shell and grows a new one. Rabbi Twerski says, 'It is the uncomfortableness that causes the impetus for growth'. He states that it is at times of stress that we enable growth. When helping people with change, Rabbi Dr Twerski states, we need to 'encourage them to have tenacity over surrender to the uncomfortableness'. It is also important that we remind ourselves that 'saving' people from the stress of change might not be in their best interest. It will keep them stuck. Stress is the necessary step towards growth; don't deny people the opportunity by stepping in and saving them, just because you can.

Our feelings are very much present in our communication. Ensuring trust and psychological safety are emerging key factors of productivity. As a manager, you need to keep your eye on the value of emotions to the growth of your direct reports, and determine how to respond to maximise the effectiveness of your conversations.

Fear

Growth doesn't happen in our comfort zone, it happens outside. In fact, it happens at the edges. But if we venture too far outside our comfort zone, we suffer anxious thoughts like, "we don't have the skills required" or, "we just can't do it". So, if your direct report has a strong fear or high avoidance, you mightn't want to start with the most challenging tasks—the amount of fear has to be 'right' and not overwhelming. Your clicking conversations will show you where the edge of the comfort zone is, and that is where you both should concentrate your efforts.

No fear

It may also be that the individual feels so safe they won't try to stretch for growth. In which case, you may need to *disturb* them comfortably with 'an empathic shove'. Sometimes I decide a person's goal precisely because they have avoided it. Then, I work alongside them to make it happen successfully. I want them to sense they have achieved something they previously hadn't thought possible. Initially they will be happy in their ability to perform the task so unexpectedly, but more importantly, they also then have a formula to continue to stretch into the uncomfortable.

If someone has become too comfortable for growth, it is an interesting conversation to have. Is that okay? Is that acceptable to both parties? Is there a blocking reason that needs to be fixed, or is everyone comfortable? What is the inspiration that is required for change? What is the information that you don't know, or they don't know? What do they want from you in terms of support? I think it is a worthy discussion to have in light of the unconscious passive pull to accept the norm.

Anger and defensiveness

Often, when we are in a conversation about another person's growth, their pride may be challenged. It can be that the individual retreats (flight) or attacks back (fight). Here we find ourselves in a clunking or a clashing conversation. The longer this conversational style exists before the growth opportunity is taken, the harder it is to return from, and the more damage is done. Don't help create the damaging game. If your direct report gets defensive, you don't need to attack or defend back. Support their feelings and decide together if they need a break from the conversation. Returning to the conversation once the emotion is more controlled will enable you to support them to use that emotion to help you both move towards a solution, rather than it blocking solution-focused thinking.

The key is not to find yourself triggered into a behaviour that keeps the clunking conversation alive. If you don't respond with anger to their anger, if you don't withdraw as a response to their withdrawal, you will move through this easier. Increasing the space between our reaction and our response is a skill to practice. This is a good thing to remember when having conversations that create growth. You will have feelings; they will have feelings. Developing a habit of pausing, even for one second, before you respond will give you a chance to screen for any unhelpful feelings that might inhibit your best response. If you need a longer pause, take it. If your feelings become too powerful to withhold, you may even decide to halt a conversation and return to it later. Acting on strong emotions, in the moment, will undermine your ability to have a conversation that creates growth.

Supporting new experiences

We can provide advice, suggestions or learnings that can support someone in their growth. Recommending books, videos, verbally explaining or visually demonstrating concepts are part of the essential support that a leading people manager will use. In addition, we will need to co-create new experiences that enable the person to grow. This might involve developing their skills by sending them on training, or taking them out on client visits or requiring them to represent you at network events. Perhaps it is working front of house so they increase their empathy for support staff, or shadowing another colleague for the day to increase their awareness of other departments. It may be that you encourage new experiences, like innovation hack sessions, or you introduce regular 3-minute breathing spaces throughout the day. Whatever your focus, it makes sense for you both to determine the key behavioural or emotional measures that you will use to track value.

Taking the time to give someone a lesson is paramount to cultivating growth. If your direct report is struggling to complete a task because there aren't enough hours in the day or there aren't enough resources to do the job, take something off them, or step in and help. Create a conversation that enables them to tell you what they need and for you to hear the ways that you could proactively help.

One of the most inspiring people managers I have ever worked with was a global executive leader. She met monthly with 52 people (one on one). She used this time to find out how she could support new experiences for them. She would open doors for people, no matter where they were in the business. She organised funding for courses, secondments or meetings; she advised on connections that would be helpful inside or outside the business; she mentored younger versions of herself, and she steered people in the right direction for their bigger or immediate goals. This not only increased the knowledge gained by each individual, but it had such strong engagement implications. She had such a profound impact on so many people. Her support was tangible and she was involved in what mattered to them. The respect, efficiency and influence she gained was immense, but that was not the driver of her behaviour—contribution to her colleagues' growth was her number one goal.

Setting up new experiences provokes a conscious or unconscious experiment and is crucial to the psychological changes involved in growth. Over 10 years ago, I contributed to a book called *Oxford Guide to Behavioural Experiments in Cognitive Therapy (Cognitive Behaviour Therapy: Science and Practice) (2004)*. The premise of the book was that experimentation is necessary for growth. Changing our perceptions and thoughts on paper is possible, but hard. What is easier for our brain to assimilate is the experience of the behavioural test.

In a behavioural test, the experiment starts with a hypothesis/prediction: what do you think will happen if you try this new experience? The second stage is doing the test and the third stage is reviewing the original prediction (see Figure 5). For example, if Tom is trying to grow in his confidence to network with high profile people, you may set up an experience that enables him to stretch. Perhaps his prediction will be that he will not have very much to say, that he will feel awkward and leave a bad impression. It may be at that point that you support him with some advice, discuss the inspiration of the networking, use some coaching methods to draw out previous successful experiences or current skills, or that you set up practical experiences such as training or give him a session in role playing. For the sake of this example, let's say that he is still left with some anxiety that he will show himself up by not being able to maintain a conversation. Once the prediction has been made, assess the strength of the prediction by asking him to give a percentage to indicate how strongly he believes it will happen. After the event, we rate the percentage again. Ideally the prediction will have shifted and that, along with the behavioural act of success, will reduce his future reticence.

In what way can you create new experiences for your direct reports that would enable their growth? How can you support their growth by providing experiences that cause perspiration, and support them through it?

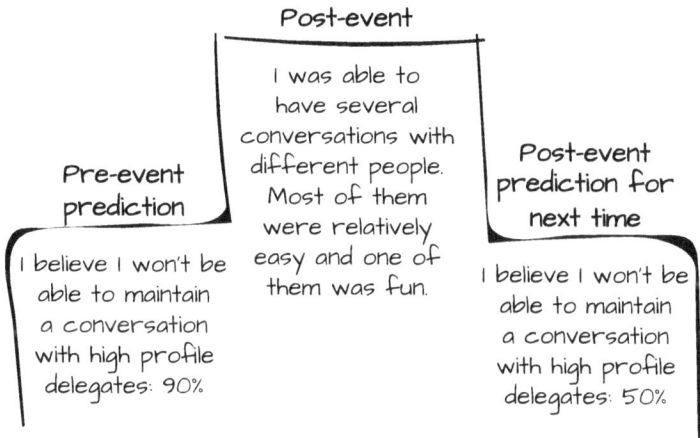

Post-event

Pre-event prediction

I believe I won't be able to maintain a conversation with high profile delegates: 90%

I was able to have several conversations with different people. Most of them were relatively easy and one of them was fun.

Post-event prediction for next time

I believe I won't be able to maintain a conversation with high profile delegates: 50%

Figure 5: Behavioural experiment

SIX

The future

Active growth is created when we have inspiration, comprehension and perspiration. Your conversations can propel the performance of your direct reports every time you meet, by keeping these central to your thinking and action. As a people manager who wants to contribute to maximising growth, help your direct reports by focusing on their why, what and how they are going to change, and determine your role in each of those phases.

Without much tweaking, this map of growth will serve you well with your clients, your own managers and with people outside of work. It will also serve you well for your own growth (I know you have been thinking about that as you have been reading). Use the methods described in here for yourself and your own growth, create measures and supports for your success, and try to move yourself one notch at a time. If you have set yourself a target of contributing to growth every time you talk, I salute you, but I also urge you to take the advice in the book about how you might best progress.

In my programs, I provide you with a diagnostic on the effectiveness of your conversations so you can really start to self-regulate and push the amount that you contribute to others. This type of self-analysis is key to your own sense of wellbeing and value, and obviously, the ripples cast wide.

Why we need growth conversations

The financial benefits of focusing on engagement and performance are enormous. The large-scale economies, which are associated with authentic, honest communication based on high quality, high quantity clicking conversations, are clear. But there is something bigger than that. We have a higher purpose to our conversations than individual or organisational growth.

Think of a person in your life who has had an incredibly positive impact on you. When you think of that person, from wherever you met them in your life, and however well you knew them, you will probably remember something they said. They made you **feel** something simply through the words they used and the time they spent with you. Conversations are powerful.

In the same way, we can see how conversations can be so superbly damaging. What conversation or phrase do you carry with you that perhaps arose from one conversation, at one point in time— nevertheless you bring it up in your head often. Conversations are powerful.

Unfortunately, I am still brought in to consult to organisations that treat their people like widgets and their clients as if they are numbers. Losing touch with people internally and externally can be a sad result of corporate life.

Bill Gates was recently interviewed about the fact that 50% of jobs done by humans today are vulnerable to replacement by robots. In the interview, he highlights that we should be celebrating the fact that this shift will be happening in our world. He says, 'human empathy and understanding are very very unique' (Chui, et al., 2016). He paints a future where robots 'taking' our jobs will free us to focus on the roles that society needs us most in, like teaching or supporting those with special needs. This maximising of our unique skills as empathic communicators is one that I truly believe to be essential. Organisations focusing on having effective conversations are future-proofing themselves.

If we want to stay relevant in times of increased automation, we need to foster and build our unique skill set. Let's get *more* human. We must get underneath the habit of surface conversations. The unspoken will undermine your progress. We must focus on trust, and we need to understand how to influence each other to achieve a sustainable future.

Every interaction you have with someone has an influence that spreads wide. If we were all willing and able to have conversations that create growth, imagine what that would look like for humanity.

Works Cited

Anon., 2013. *Start with why.* s.l.: TED.

Chui, M., Manyika, J. & Miremadi, M., 2016. Where machines could replace humans—and where they can't (yet). *McKinsey & Company*, July.

Cook, P., 2013. *The rules of management: How to revolutionise productivity, innovation and engagement by implementing projects that matter.* s.l.: Wiley.

Deloitte, 2016. Crunch time: Finance in a digital world.

Dolan, G., 2017. *Stories for work: The essential guide to business storytelling.* s.l.: Wiley.

Duckworth, A., 2016. *Grit: The power of passion and perseverance.* s.l.: Scribner.

Dweck, D. C., 2012. *Mindset: Changing the way you think to fulfil your potential.* s.l.: Robinson.

Ferris, T., 2007. *The 4-hour Work Week.* US: Crown Publishing Group.

Gallup, 2017. *Gallup 2017 Global Emotions Report,* s.l.: s.n.

Gladwell, M., 2008. *Outliers: The story of success.* s.l.: Litle, Brown and Company.

Hays, 2017. *Press releases.* [Online]
Available at: https://www.hays.com.au/press-releases/
HAYS_1812340
[Accessed 31 July 2017].

Karpman M.D., S. B., 1968. Fairy tales and script drama analysis. *Transactional Analysis Bulletin,* 26(7), pp. 39-43.

Lambert, S., 2000. *Faking It.* UK: Channel 4.

McCann Worldgroup, n.d. *Scribd.* [Online]
Available at: https://www.scribd.com/doc/56263899/
McCann-Worldgroup-Truth-About-Youth
[Accessed 31 July 2017].

Miller, W. R. & Rollnick, S., 2012. *Motivational Interviewing.* s.l.: Guilford Publications.

Molinaro, V., 2016. *The leadership contract: The fine print to becoming an accountable leader.* s.l.: Wiley.

OnDemand, C., 2013. *Employee report,* s.l.: s.n.

Paul Dr., R. & Elder Dr., L., 2006. *Critical Thinking.* [Online]
Available at: https://www.criticalthinking.org/TGS_
files/SocraticQuestioning2006.pdf

Pink, D., 2011. *Drive: The surprising truth about what motivates us.* s.l.:Riverhead Books.

Prochaska, J. O. & DiClimente, C. C., 1984. *The transtheoretical approach: Towards a systematic eclectic framework.* USA: Dow Jones Irwin.

Taleb, N. N., 2014. *Antifragile: Things that gain form disorder (incerto).* s.l.: Random House.

Twerski, R. D. A., n.d. *Rabbi Dr. Abraham Twerski on responding to stress.* s.l.: Jinsider via YouTube.

Zenger, J. & Folkman, J., 2017. How to improve at work when you're not getting feedback. *Harvard Business review*, 09 May.

About the author

Amy is obsessed with finding triggers that lead to sustainable growth. Her deep understanding of human communication enables powerful activation. She believes we have a responsibility to enable growth in others, to close the gap between potential and performance.

She speaks, authors and mentors on how to grow powerfully. She works with her clients to give programs that go deeper than the surface to find the people triggers of true and sustainable growth.

Amy shows organisations how to have effective conversations that activate growth. To find out more about this, please see www.DrAmySilver.com. Sign up to her regular *Silverlinings*, where she posts tips and tricks for activating growth, and connecting to self and others. You can find out about upcoming public offers and downloadable resources.

Please also keep this conversation going by writing to her and her team directly at hello@DrAmySilver.com.

www.ingramcontent.com/pod-product-compliance
Lightning Source LLC
Chambersburg PA
CBHW070356200326
41518CB00012B/2246